The Merchant Navy

No trades deserve so much care to procure, and preserve, and encouragement to prosecute, as those that employ the most shipping.

Sir Josiah Child (1630–99)

The Merchant Navy

Ronald Hope

STANFORD MARITIME LONDON

Acknowledgments

More than 100 good people in the shipping industry have helped to make this work accurate. To ensure that no error appeared in Chapter 5 Mr. R. A. H. Tucker of the Department of Trade went well beyond the call of duty. To him and to all the others I am most grateful.

R.H.

Stanford Maritime Limited
Member Company of the George Philip Group
12–14 Long Acre London WC2E 9LP
Editor D Nicolson

First published in Great Britain 1980

Printed by Ebenezer Baylis & Son Limited
Worcester and London

British Library Cataloguing in Publication Data
Hope, Ronald
The Merchant Navy.
1. Shipping – Great Britain – History
I. Title
387.5'0941 HE823

ISBN 0 540 07335 0

Contents

1 The Merchant Seaman Down the Ages

Hardy he was, and wise to undertake;
With many a tempest had his beard been shake.
Geoffrey Chaucer

'Some of my neighbours', wrote Edward Barlow three hundred years ago, 'would not venture a day's journey from out of the smoke of their chimneys or the taste of their mother's milk'.

Barlow himself had little time for people like these, for he wanted to see strange places and new things. At the age of fifteen he ran away to sea, and such a greenhorn was he that he did not even know the sea was salt. Nevertheless, he struggled to educate himself–he could not write when he first left home–and he was not satisfied until he was in command of a ship.

Down the ages there have been thousands of British boys with Barlow's yearning for high adventure. There may have been some as long ago as 1,500BC, for it is quite likely that at about that time the blue stones of Stonehenge were brought by sea from Pembrokeshire in Wales to Salisbury Plain in England . Certainly by 55BC, when Julius Caesar first brought his Roman legions across the English Channel, some of those who lived in Britain were no strangers to the sea. In an age when the Romans preferred to use oars, the British were out sailing on the deep, and the seas of north-west Europe which they sailed were rougher than any Roman seas.

Four hundred years later still, Celtic seafarers from Ireland were venturing into the Atlantic ocean. They had discovered Iceland, and may have discovered America, long before any Vikings set sail for those parts. They knew the Norwegian coast, and it is more than probable that they taught the Vikings themselves how to navigate upon the oceans.

From the Anglo-Saxon poem *The Seafarer* it is clear that before the Vikings appeared in British waters those who lived in England, as well as those who lived in Ireland, were well acquainted with the sea. 'For pastime the gannet's cry served me', sang the Anglo-Saxon poet; and to prove that he was an ancestor worthy of Edward Barlow, the boy who ran away to sea, he went on: 'Desire in my heart ever urges my spirit to wander, to seek out the home of the stranger in lands afar off'.

From all this we see that five hundred years before the Phoenicians were towing the cedars of Lebanon down to Tel Aviv to build King Solomon's temple, British seafarers may have towed some of the Stonehenge stones along the Welsh coast, a much more dangerous journey; and five hundred years before the Vikings met King Alfred's ships in battle, Celtic seafarers were sailing well out into the Atlantic. There is no doubt that the British seafaring tradition is as old as any in the world.

The Laws of Oléron

It was in the wine trade from Bordeaux, a trade in which P&O is still engaged, that many British seamen learned their jobs. Indeed British seafarers brought wines to the site of Three Quays, right by the Tower of London, for close on two thousand years; and it is in this trade that we first learn something of the men themselves, for it was to regulate the wine trade that the Laws of Oléron were devised.

Oléron is an island off the west coast of France, not far from the region which produces some of the world's finest wines, and in the middle ages Oléron was a centre of trade. The decisions made there by the wise men who were called upon to settle disputes were collected–some say by King Richard of England–to represent the 'good uses and customs of the sea'. In these medieval ships, ships not much bigger than barges, the master was a leader of men but he was not a law unto himself. When a ship was ready to sail the Laws of Oléron decreed that the master should 'take council with his fellows and say, "Mates, how like ye this weather?" Some will say, "It is not good, let it pass". Others will say, "The weather is good and fair". The master ought to agree to the most, or else if the ship perish he is bound to restore the value as it is apprised, if he have the wherewithal'.

This seems pleasantly democratic and suggests that where ignorance was bliss it was folly to be wise. However, the law gave the master the authority and the means to keep order. For telling lies at the table the sailor was fined fourpence; or eightpence if the lie were told to the master himself. The master could strike a member of the crew once, but if he did it again the seaman could hit him back; if the seaman struck first he was to lose his hand or pay a fine equal to about one-half of his wages for a trip to Bordeaux. How many hands were valued at less than five shillings, one wonders? Perhaps hands and crew were sometimes synonymous in medieval times.

The system of wages then prevailing in western Europe–and, indeed, prevailing for some centuries afterwards–gave the seaman a fixed wage and also a small portion of the ship's cargo capacity. This latter he could use either to trade with on his own account or to hire out to a merchant, and the master was required to consult the crew on their decision: 'Mates will ye freight by yourselves, or be allowed at the freight of the ship'. To freight by oneself could be a risky business (as Barlow discovered in the 17th century), but it could also be a profitable one, and on the whole the medieval seaman seemed to make as much money as the highest-paid artisans ashore. Advances of wages were made at this time as they are now; indeed it would seem that the mariner received all his wages in advance, one-half before sailing and one-half at the loading port to enable him to trade on his own account.

Victualling scales were also laid down after a fashion, though it appears that the men were more concerned about their liquor than they were about their meat. Norman sailors, who came from cider country, insisted on two meals a day because they had no wine; but Breton sailors, who enjoyed wine on their voyages had rights to only one meal. When the cargo itself was wine the men believed that they were entitled to a double ration on feast-days, and we know from Chaucer, whose job it was to collect customs payments in London, that seamen sometimes broached the cargo.

Up to the time of the great oceanic discoveries at the end of the fifteenth century seafarers had much in common with the communities still to be found in small fishing ports. Voyages were relatively short and usually carried out within sight of land, most of them being made in the summer months. Food and drink were readily available and there was then no problem of scurvy, starvation and the extreme physical discomfort of later voyages; nor was the harsh discipline of later centuries necessary to force men to endure such conditions. Nevertheless, there was the ever-present danger of piracy so that the seafarer had to be a sturdy fellow, able to defend himself. Chaucer's shipman was a fine seaman who knew every harbour from Gotland to Finisterre and every creek in Brittany and Spain, but if he fought and won a battle at sea he sometimes sent his adversaries to a watery grave with no more than very rough justice.

The maritime powers

In medieval times England was not the great maritime power she was to become. The Italian city states of Venice and Genoa dominated the trade from the Mediterranean and their vessels were familiar in northern waters long before the first official record of the Flanders galleys in 1317. These galleys from Venice, although remaining under the command of a state-appointed captain, were hired to traders, and preparations for the annual convoy, which varied in size from two to five ships, began in January. Their route took them by way of Cape d'Istria, Corfu, Otranto, Syracuse, Messina, Naples, Majorca, and the coasts of Spain and Morocco, to Lisbon and Rye. At Rye the galleys bound for Flanders separated from those bound for England. The English ports of call were Sandwich, London and Southampton, and those on the Continent were Sluys, Middleburg and Antwerp. The vessels met again at Sandwich in time to avoid autumnal gales on the way home.

These and the Genoese vessels brought the spices and silks of the East (collected at Trebizond, Constantinople, Damascus, Aleppo, Alexandria and Cairo), the currants of Greece, cotton, and Italian glass and earthenware. In return they were customers for British wool and woven cloth, among this cloth being the Lincoln green worn by Robin Hood and his men. The galleys were mainly propelled by oars, each of them carrying 180 oarsmen, and the long pull seems to have given them a thirst for one reads of the oarsmen pledging themselves beyond their pay in the taverns of London and Bruges and being redeemed by their captains.

The maritime laws of Venice reflect an interest in shipping affairs comparable with our own. Limits of length, breadth and depth for vessels of various size were laid down and compliance with these regulations presumably entailed official inspection during building as it does today. Other statutes specified the number of sails, anchors and cables; ballasting, stowage and the carriage of deck cargoes; and the assignment of loading marks and a manning scale.

In northern Europe another maritime power dominated the trade routes. The Hanseatic League, well established by the middle of the 13th century, was a confederation of German trading towns which included Lübeck, Bremen and Hamburg, and its power was based on its control over the herring fishery. In medieval times a supply of salted fish was necessary to comply with the rules of the Church concerning fast-days: Friday was the day for fish even then. For two months every year the Scania peninsula in the south-west corner of Sweden was the centre of the fishing industry and a thriving market. The Hansa left the catching of the fish to the Danes and Swedes and concentrated on salting and distributing it; a profitable sideline consisted of supplying the needs of the thousands of men who temporarily occupied the peninsula.

Hanseatic vessels distributed fish to Germany, Russia, Poland, other Baltic states, Flanders, England, France, Spain and Portugal. The return cargoes produced further opportunities to trade and the Hanseatic merchants became the middlemen and carriers for the whole of northern Europe. Wherever they traded they set up 'factories' or depots and they were ruthless in their attempts to keep this trade entirely in their own hands. From Russia they obtained hides, skins, tallow, furs, honey and wax, the latter being used for candles. Also by way of Russia came Chinese and Persian silks. From Scandinavia came iron, copper and building stone, and grain was shipped from Poland and Russia to the Low Countries and even to England. Perhaps most important of all was the Hanseatic control of the raw materials of shipbuilding–timber and tar–from the Baltic and Scandinavian countries, for this made other maritime nations heavily dependent upon them.

The Hanseatic merchants found it necessary to supplement earlier maritime laws and their later trade was governed by special decrees issued by the council of the League. The master and his crew became hired servants, and it was a capital offence for a man to jump ship after he had received an advance of pay. Victualling scales mention the issue of beef or bacon, peas and 'boiled dishes' on meat days, and salt fish, gruel, beans and peas on other days.

The League was firmly entrenched in Britain and had its principal factory at the London Steelyard situated where Cannon Street station now is. For a time the League took the lion's share in the trade in British woollens–a financial help to the English kings, but a cause of restiveness among the merchants of the City of London and a hindrance to the development of the British Merchant Navy.

Modern seafarers are familiar with the scallop shell which symbolises the tankers of the Shell fleet. Marcus Samuel, founder of that company, is said to have drawn his inspiration from the ornaments decorated with sea-shells which his father sold in Victorian days, but such ornamentation had its origin in religious custom and the scallop shell is the symbol of St James. Before the last war, children in the ports of London and Bristol still displayed the scallop shell in the 'grottoes' or wild flower displays with which they celebrated St James's day, and doubtless they did so in medieval times when English pilgrim ships sailed to the shrine of St James of Compostella in Northern Spain.

A fifteenth-century poem commemorates the sailing of the pilgrim ships, with their sea-sick passengers and robust seafarers: the master calls for a pot of beer while the pilgrims read their Bibles, and the poet vividly recalls the stink of the bilge-water which–as that seafaring poet laureate John Masefield pointed out–at least indicates that the ship was sound. English seafarers of the time were not averse to a little piracy on their own account and made an unsuccessful attempt to capture the Flemish galleys in 1488, an event which did not seem much to concern the king for he suggested on that occasion that a pot of wine might put the matter right.

It was indeed difficult to know where to draw the line between piracy and naval action. Naval ships were largely requisitioned merchantmen and in time of national emergency a large part of the merchant fleet would be withdrawn for the king's service. It was a mode of life which produced the competent, flexible and audacious sailor who was shortly to establish British maritime supremacy.

The world expands

The end of the fifteenth and the beginning of the sixteenth century witnessed the great voyages of discovery which opened the ocean routes to trade. The impetus came from Portugal and much of the credit must be given to Prince Henry, called Henry the Navigator, the grandson of the English John of Gaunt and very much an Englishman in appearance. To realise his ambitions Henry set about producing better ships and better means of navigating them. He improved the caravel so that it could sail safely beyond the Mediterranean and, although in his lifetime his captains did not penetrate beyond Gambia, subsequent expeditions penetrated farther and farther down the African coast until, in 1486, Bartholomew Diaz rounded the Cape of Good Hope and, in 1498, Vasco da Gama reached Calicut on the coast of India. In the meantime, Christopher Columbus, a Genoese pilot who had vainly tried to persuade Henry VII to employ him before he found favour with King Ferdinand of Spain, had arrived in the West Indies. In 1492, of course, Columbus thought that he had arrived in the Far East and the existence of a 'New World' remained unsuspected for nearly a generation. In 1497 John Cabot also made a voyage to the new world from Bristol, making his American landfall in the region of Newfoundland or Nova Scotia.

These events, together with the closing by the Turks of the old caravan routes to the East, shifted the balance of power from the Mediterranean Sea to the Atlantic seaboard. The Pope divided the world across the oceans between Spain and Portugal but, though enterprising, these nations were also extravagant. Much of the treasure which they obtained by plunder in the New World was mortgaged in advance as security for loans from the merchant bankers of the Low Countries. Some of it was also plundered from the Spanish treasure fleets by French, English and Dutch adventurers who proved, in the long run, more able in ordinary commercial ventures.

In England men were on the alert. Henry VIII established a navy to protect English shipping and, by the middle of the 16th century, English ships were trading as far afield as Iceland and the eastern Mediterranean and adventurous seafarers were trying to find either a north-west or a north-east passage which would bypass the Portuguese road to the Indies.

One of these seafarers was Martin Frobisher, a Yorkshireman of Welsh descent who was one of the more successful of the early Arctic voyagers. Frobisher thought he could find a way across the top of the world and saw possibilities in a trade with Canada. People with money provided him with three cockleshells of ships, two vessels each of 20tons burden and a pinnace of only 10tons, and this little fleet sailed in the summer of 1576. The pinnace was soon lost in a storm and never heard of again, and not long afterwards the other vessel deserted. However, Frobisher pushed on and, after sighting Greenland, nearly lost his own ship in a storm which pushed her over on her beam ends. Still he was not deterred. At the end of July he sighted Resolution Island, and in the middle of August he landed on an island in Frobisher Bay–or Strait, as he believed it to be–where he and his men met some apparently friendly Eskimoes. One of the Eskimoes agreed by means of signs to pilot them into those western seas which Frobisher believed to be so readily accessible, but he wished to go ashore to prepare himself. Frobisher sent him off in one of his boats with a crew of five men, but these men disobeyed their instructions to land the Eskimo within sight of the ship and they were never seen again. Frobisher made repeated attempts to recover his men and even managed to capture another Eskimo as hostage but all in vain. A week or so after landing, he and his thirteen remaining men decided to return to England.

In the meantime other Englishmen were adventuring in other directions. Frobisher himself had voyaged with John Hawkins who had followed up his father's tentative attempts to join in the trade to Africa and Brazil. While voyaging to the Canary Islands, Hawkins had learned that negroes were good merchandise in the West Indies, and, although the Spanish government was anxious to keep this trade in its own hands, the Spanish colonists were often ready to buy where they could. Hawkins found it a lucrative trade at first but the third expedition in 1567 proved disastrous, for the Spaniards attacked his fleet while it lay repairing in Vera Cruz harbour. Only two of the six ships escaped but, fortunately for British maritime history, Hawkins and his kinsman, Francis Drake, were of their crews.

The slave trade was odious, but in caring for the welfare of his crews Hawkins was enlightened and he recognised the value of good provisions on a long voyage. Biscuit, barrels of meal, beans and peas, hogsheads of beef, flitches of bacon, stockfish (dried and salted cod), ling, beer, cider, Malmsey, vinegar, oil, honey and aniseed: these were among the stores he took, and he procured fresh food whenever he could. On one voyage, of a total complement of 170, he lost only thirteen members of his crew by way of disease, and this was remarkably few for the time. The chances of returning home from an oceanic voyage in the days of the first Queen Elizabeth cannot have been much more than one in five.

It is sometimes forgotten, not least by naval historians, that the Royal Navy exists only to protect the Merchant Navy, and in war it is the Merchant Navy that suffers most and the men of the Merchant Navy who sacrifice most. It is appropriate therefore that Drake, the man who made the British navy a successful instrument of war, should have been a merchant seaman. A brilliant piece of leadership and a remarkable feat of navigation, his voyage round the world between 1577 and 1580, was also a very successful privateering and trading enterprise which gave its backers handsome returns. Eight years later, although Lord Effingham was in command of the English fleet at the time, it is Drake's name that one remembers as vanquisher of the Armada. Up to that time the ships which took part in the great sea battles were moved by oarsmen and fought by soldiers. But, first and foremost, Drake and his English contemporaries were neither oarsmen nor soldiers; they were seamen.

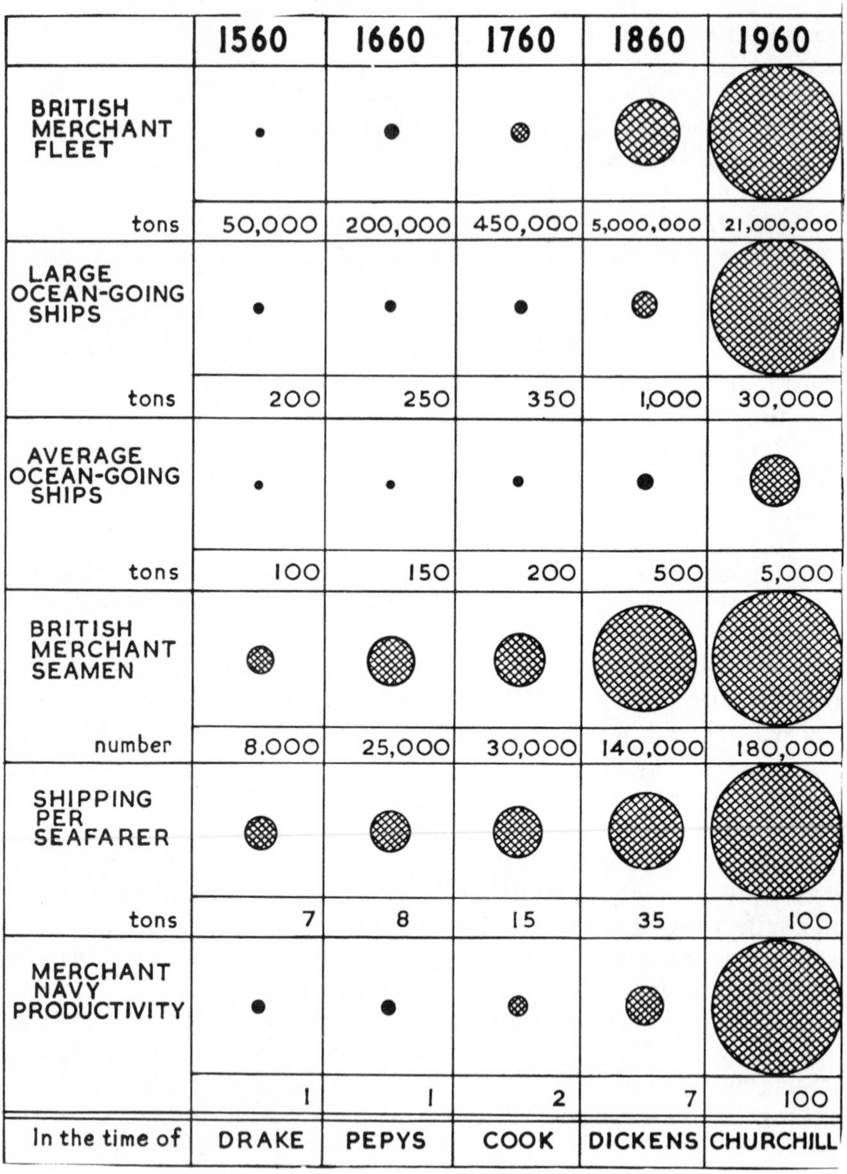

	1560	1660	1760	1860	1960
BRITISH MERCHANT FLEET tons	50,000	200,000	450,000	5,000,000	21,000,000
LARGE OCEAN-GOING SHIPS tons	200	250	350	1,000	30,000
AVERAGE OCEAN-GOING SHIPS tons	100	150	200	500	5,000
BRITISH MERCHANT SEAMEN number	8.000	25,000	30,000	140,000	180,000
SHIPPING PER SEAFARER tons	7	8	15	35	100
MERCHANT NAVY PRODUCTIVITY	1	1	2	7	100
In the time of	DRAKE	PEPYS	COOK	DICKENS	CHURCHILL

Fig 1 Five centuries of change
Since 1960 British tonnage has increased to 27 million tons gross (the peak figure was 33 million tons in 1975), and the number of seafarers manning the fleet, including those living outside the United Kingdom, has fallen to 81,500. Shipping tons per seafarer have trebled in these 20 years.

Trade with the East

The history of the Merchant Navy in the 17th and 18th centuries is closely associated with the rise and prosperity of the East India Company, forerunner of the modern P&O. The formation of such chartered companies was encouraged by the Crown because it found itself unable to provide the navy necessary to protect England's growing trade and this was a means of letting the burden fall upon the merchants.

The Dutch and the French also had companies trading with the East and for a long time the Dutch company was the most powerful of the three, for in the 17th century Holland had better financial resources than either of her rivals. 'John Company', as the English company came to be known later in its history, eventually added India to Britain's oversea possessions. In the meantime many a young man made his fortune in the company's service, and many more died of disease in foreign parts. Seamen, on the whole, rarely made their fortunes, though many died of disease.

The journal kept by Captain Nicholas Downton of the *Peppercorn* describes one voyage of this period, a voyage from Bantam in Java to Waterford in Ireland which was made in 1613. It is not untypical of many others.

Shortly after sailing on 7th February the ship was found to be leaking, and this was owing to negligence on the part of the company's own shipwrights. Apparently the vessel had never been loaded so deeply before and the faulty workmanship had been above the waterline. On the day the leak developed the ship's minister died, and this was the first of twenty deaths to occur on the homeward voyage. When the ship sailed from Java many of the crew had been suffering from dysentery, and this was one of the diseases that took its toll.

Before arriving in Table Bay on 10th May the ship was damaged in a storm, and set on fire through the carelessness of a drunken cook; all the ship's gunpowder was spoiled by heavy seas shipped aboard, and the Cape of Good Hope was overshot in consequence of using faulty instruments. Worse was to come. Captain Downton had hoped to find fresh water and greenstuff to combat the scurvy at St Helena, but he found only two unfriendly Portuguese vessels, and discretion forced him to stand on. As they neared home the crew grew progressively weaker, but the universal fear of pirates prevented other vessels from recognising their plight and, in desperation after another storm, Downton took the ship into Waterford. The journey had so far taken seven months.

Although far from well, Downton wrote to London for fresh stores and 'ten honest sailors' to bring the ship round to London. He dared not trust the twenty-six survivors of his crew, for one had already caused a mutiny on the homeward voyage and another, charged with piratical intentions while in Waterford, managed to get Dowton himself arrested briefly on the same charge.

Later in this century Edward Barlow sometimes rued the day that he ran away to sea. He was an apprentice on his first ship but his cabin, he said, was 'much like to some gentleman's dog-kennel', and he had not been aboard long before, by accident, he was knocked down the hold and fractured his skull. Fortunately he was thickheaded as he was obstinate and, over the years, his cracked head bothered him less than the indifferent quality of the food in nearly all the ships in which he served. At his uncle's house in London he had turned up his nose at some salted meat, but he would have been glad enough of it many times afterwards. If they were any length of time at sea the crew were invariably put on short rations and the passage below is typical of many in Barlow's journal:

'We were now forced to go to one quart of beverage to one man a day, which beverage was made of sour wine and stinking water, which was very hard with us; and the weather being hot and always eating salt victuals, I could not get my belly full, which made me often repent of my going to sea, . . . I was always thinking that beggars had a far better life of it and lived better than I did'.

Elsewhere in the journal he describes his Christmas of that same year. There was no roast beef and Christmas pudding on board ship as there would be for the folks at home, but–writes Barlow–'a little bit of Irish beef for four men, which had lain in pickle two or three years and was as rusty as the Devil, with a little stinking oil or butter which was all colours of the rainbow, many men in England greasing their cartwheels with better'. Nor was this Christmas Day a holiday for deckboy Barlow, for he had to work all day and part of the night.

Conditions did not change much on the great ocean routes over a period of two hundred years. On his first exploratory voyage from 1768 to 1771 Captain Cook lost much the same proportion of his crew as Captain Downton had in 1613, returning to England with only fifty-six men of a total complement of ninety-four, many of these men dying of dysentery on the same run home from Java. As early as the 17th century it was realised that the other great scourge of all ocean-going seamen, scurvy, was attributable to a lack of fresh food, and enlightened commanders like Cook not only obtained fresh food when they could but experimented with such portable sources of vitamins as sauerkraut, 'marmalade of carrots' and 'inspissated juice of wort and beer'. Yet it was not until the 19th century that scurvy was eradicated by the regular provision of fruit juice.

It is true that the sailor enjoyed some compensations for his hard life at sea. All the pretty girls flocked round Barlow on one of the rare occasions when he came home in a fine new suit and with sixteen pounds in his pocket, and he enjoyed savouring strange foods, drinking new wines, and the many other exotic experiences which came to him abroad. Sailing ships were often becalmed, or made little progress in light winds, and at such times it was sometimes possible to obtain fresh fish from the sea. Ships carried livestock–chickens, sheep and pigs–for some part of the voyage, and Dr Samuel Johnson wrote a Latin epigram in honour of the goat which went twice round the world with Wallis and Cook to provide milk for 'the gentlemen's coffee'. Captain William Keeling, master of the East Indiaman *Dragon*, records as early as 1608 that he had Shakespeare's tragedy *Hamlet* acted aboard his ship 'to keep my people from idleness and unlawful games, or sleep', and there was usually some skylarking when the line was crossed. Describing a voyage to India round about 1770, William Hickey, who was no mean judge, found the food very good, except that no bread was baked on board and biscuit had to take its place; and on another occasion he warmly commended dolphin as a dish–'when dressed in the American manner, that is, cut in slices with layers of pork and vegetables, and well stewed'.

The press-gang

During the 17th century the British were frequently at war with the Dutch. During the 18th century the British were frequently at war with the French. Broadly speaking these were trade wars, largely fought upon the sea, and the merchant seaman was in the thick of them. Until the end of the 18th century the Dutch remained the greatest maritime power even though they were not by then so cock-a-hoop as they had been in Barlow's time when, as he commented, their boasting and bragging was 'heartburning to a true-hearted Englishman'. During these long years every sail that appeared over the horizon was a potential enemy and until the home port was reached no seafarer could consider himself safe. Indeed he was not safe then, for at home there was the very real prospect of capture by the press-gang and a period of enforced service in the Navy.

As always in time of emergency, the Navy fell back upon the merchantman. In time of war there were never enough trained men to man both the merchant service and the Navy. In peacetime every merchant ship had to take apprentices, and the guardians of the poor were directed by an act of Queen Anne's time to send pauper boys to sea. At its worst the system was not far removed from slavery and it was a convenient means of disposing of unwanted boys from the age of ten upwards. Not, of course, that all apprentices were poor boys 'on the parish'. Captain Cook–apart from Drake, the most distinguished of all merchant seamen–was a voluntary apprentice in the merchant service, and the government offered bounties to the professional merchant seaman if he transferred to the Navy. Cook accepted such an offer, partly because he saw opportunities for advancement, and partly because the press-gang would have had him anyway.

The press-gang worked both in port and at sea, and those subject to the press were rogues, vagabonds and sailors–preferably the latter. When the press worked a port the local authorities were called upon to co-operate, soldiers were employed, and the press, under the command of a commissioned officer to make it a lawful attempt upon the liberty of the subject, searched all the hiding places. Not surprisingly public sympathy was often with the sailor and he did not have to give himself up. He was entitled to run, or even fight, for his liberty, and in a seaport many of the local worthies were connected with shipping and not altogether anxious that merchant seamen should become too scarce. It followed from all this that trained seamen were most effectively secured at sea and the press-gang was authorised to take all the seamen it required from any homecoming merchantman provided enough were left on board to man the ship. Barlow was caught in this way after his seven-year apprenticeship, and he was not then allowed ashore from His Majesty's frigate *Yarmouth* for seven months for fear that he might run away. This was why some homeward bound merchantmen were abandoned by their crews when some way off their port and scratch crews had to be sent by the owners to bring the vessel in.

Although the trained seaman had some prospect of promotion in the Navy, the Navy did not pay so well as the merchant service in time of war and it was never certain when naval pay would be forthcoming. Once in the Navy a seaman might serve for years without receiving a penny either for himself or his family, and since men were disinclined to accept such conditions willingly one naval officer suggested Merchant Navy wages should be reduced to redress the balance. In time of war merchant shipowners and masters were often prepared to bargain for the men they needed, and even bribe them to desert another ship. Abroad, seamen would desert from a newly arrived ship and take jobs at higher wages in ships ready to sail. Advances of wages were sometimes made to such deserters by their new employers and monthly allowances to their families were promised during the period of their absence from home. An act passed in the reign of George III tried to put a stop to these practices, with no more success than that enjoyed by many other acts of Parliament passed at the time.

It is said that during World War I the Admiralty had to rediscover the usefulness of sending ships to sea in convoy so that they might be more easily protected from enemy attack. If so, the naval men of that day did not know their history for in times of danger ships have sailed in convoy from the earliest days of merchantmen. But forming a large convoy of sailing ships was no easy business and it sometimes took months to accomplish. The fast ship–as in more modern times–was at a disadvantage, since the speed of a convoy is the speed of the slowest ship, and although fines were levied on vessels that left the convoy, owners often preferred to pay the fine when there was the opportunity of arriving first with a new season's cargo. But the likelihood of capture was thus increased, and the danger was always greatest nearest home. The merchantman, of course, was armed and would fight for his life; the smart East Indiaman, indeed, was scarcely less well-armed than the warship; at any time these ships were as ready for a fight as that noble armed merchant cruiser, the *Jervis Bay*, when she set out to battle with the German pocket battleship *von Scheer*, on November 5th, 1940.

Another feature of sea life in these centuries was the privateer. These vessels sailed under letters of marque issued by the Admiralty and thus constituted a kind of private navy from which, with luck, the shareholders might make considerable profits. For the most part it was a dubious business, not much better than piracy, and it tended to bring out the worst side of the men engaged in it, for mutiny was not uncommon; but privateering played a significant part in the French Revolutionary and Napoleonic wars from 1793 to 1815, and the vessels built for this purpose compared very favourably in both size and armament with regular naval vessels. The French were particularly adept at the business and the approaches to the Channel were thick with friend and foe alike. The privateer did not always get the best of a fight and, with luck, a captured vessel might be recaptured. Nevertheless, it has been estimated that some 11,000 British ships of varying sizes were captured during these years, and captured merchant seamen were liable to the most unpleasant confinement until the end of the war.

The coming of steam

The activities of the press-gang did not come to an end until well after the Napoleonic wars but, by 1853, when continuous service was introduced into the Royal Navy, a new era was beginning to dawn both for British shipping and for the British merchant seaman.

The British emerged victorious from the Napoleonic wars and ships had grown bigger. An East Indiaman might now measure 1,200 tons against the 400-ton ship of a century before, but most merchantmen were still no more than 400 or 500 tons and the average size was smaller still. There had been little improvement in design for two hundred years and, although victory was sweet, the condition of the Merchant Navy was not a healthy one. In part this was because it had been built up under a system of monopoly and the protection of navigation laws which largely reserved British trade for British ships. As trade increased after the industrial revolution these laws were found to restrict competition and to promote inefficiency. Recognising that this was so, the government began to repeal these laws–often against the wishes of the shipowners of that time–and this task was completed in 1849.

In the meantime the United States had thrown out a challenge to British shipping. During the British wars against France the United States had emerged as an effective and enterprising maritime power. Her ships and manner of running them had established new standards of smartness and the term 'Yankee' had suddenly become associated with a brisk and sometimes reckless manner which was much admired. Furthermore, American ship-owners had sensed the value of speed in an age of competition and in the transatlantic trade established regular schedules with guaranteed sailing days. Hitherto ships had sailed when full of cargo, a process which might take weeks or even months.

Although the true 'clipper' came only towards the end of the period of American superiority, American ship design was an improvement over the British until the 1860's when British yards began to turn out those elegant ships of legend, *Taeping*, *Ariel*, *Thermopylae* and *Cutty Sark*, ships of 800 or 900 tons, nearly six times as long as they were wide, all of them striving to be first home with the new season's tea from China. However, by this time British superiority had again been established, not because of the building of the clippers but because the British were already building ocean-going steamships and the Americans had entered upon the American civil war. During the American civil war, from 1861 to 1865, the Confederate vessel *Alabama* alone destroyed 100,000 tons of Yankee shipping and American owners found it safer to transfer their vessels to other flags.

If historians were asked to name the significant features of the years 1789, 1805 and 1812 respectively they would probably answer that the first year marked the outbreak of the French Revolution, the second Nelson's victory over the French at the Battle of Trafalgar, and the third Napoleon's retreat from Moscow. For the merchant seaman, however, the significance of these dates is that in 1789 William Symington first built a steamship for Patrick Miller of Edinburgh; in 1805 Robert Fulton, using a British engine and boiler, ran a steamboat on the river Hudson; and in 1812 Henry Bell launched his 25-ton steamboat *Comet* on the Clyde. The British engineer thus established the supremacy of British shipping, and in 1826 the General Steam Navigation Company put steamships regularly on the run to Oporto, Lisbon and Gibraltar. Eleven years later the firm of Willcox & Anderson secured a government contract to deliver mail to Gibraltar once a month, a contract which was extended to Alexandria in 1840, and in this way established the great Peninsular and Oriental Steam Navigation Company, or P&O.

Other mail contracts were secured by the Cunard Steam-Ship Company, Royal Mail Lines and the Pacific Steam Navigation Company, and by 1840 a number of genuine steamships had crossed the Atlantic–Samuel Cunard's *Royal William* in 1833, the Irish Channel steamer *Sirius*, Brunel's *Great Western* and the City of Dublin Steam Packet Company's *Royal William* and

Liverpool, all in 1838. In July,1840, Cunard's *Britannia* first sailed with the mails from Liverpool to Halifax and Boston.

In 1856, the year before the Union Steamship Company (forerunner of the once renowned Union-Castle Line) was also awarded a mail contract, the Pacific Steam Navigation Company added to their fleet two new ships fitted with a compound engine designed by Elder and Randolph. This engine greatly improved the efficiency of the steam engine and it was further improved in 1862 by Alfred Holt of Liverpool who, a year or two later, put steamers into the China trade and founded the famous Blue Funnel Line.

In one form or another all these early companies have persisted–General Steam in P&O, Royal Mail and Pacific Steam in the Furness Withy Group , Union-Castle in British & Commonwealth, and Blue Funnel in Ocean Transport & Trading.

Crimps and coffin-ships

These tremendous changes in technique were paralleled by changes in the seafarer's way of life. In the years immediately after the Napoleonic wars there was much that was wrong with the merchant seaman. A government committee set up in 1836 to inquire into the causes of wrecks uncovered some unpleasant facts. Masters were all too often incompetent and their knowledge of navigation inadequate. There were no standards of professional competence, and almost anyone could be given a command; there was an instance of a boy of fourteen being given a command, and another of a shipowner who made a porter from his warehouse captain of one of his vessels. The committee reported that 'drunkenness, either in the master, officers or men, is a frequent cause of ships being wrecked, leading often to improper and contradictory orders on the part of the officers; sleeping on lookout or at the helm among the men occasioning ships to run foul of each other at night, and one or both foundering'. Harbours were unsuitable, lighthouses few, and navigation badly practised. Charts were often inadequate, even where vessels were provided with them, and there were no professional examinations.

Little was done about all this at the time but, after further investigation and much public criticism, the government passed the Mercantile Marine Act of 1850, which established a marine department in the Board of Trade (now the Department of Trade), made the examination of masters and mates on foreign-going vessels compulsory, and set up Mercantile Marine Offices to superintend the contracts made between shipowners and seamen. This latter provision was a blow aimed at the crimping system, though it was many years before the crimps finally found themselves out of business.

The crimps were usually keepers of somewhat dubious lodging-houses who catered for, and played upon, the weaknesses of men who had returned from months of confinement in the far from luxurious vessels of the 19th century. The crimp's aim was to separate the seaman from his pay, to find him another ship, and to pocket the advance of wages which the man would draw in discharge of the debts which the crimp had induced him to incur. 'But I'll take yer advance and I'll give yiz a chance and I'll send yiz to sea once more'–so runs a shanty of the period in which a crimp was being 'generous' to an unfortunate seaman who had lost all his money. In circumstances like these the sailor had little choice and his advance note would be 'cracked' at a high discount.

Often enough, of course, the seafarer himself behaved foolishly but the crimp and his associates gave the crews of newly arrived ships little opportunity of avoiding them. They would board the ships and practically drag seafarers ashore to their establishments. Sometimes while the seamen were still working aloft the crimp and his men would remove their baggage to the lodging-house so that the seamen had no option but to follow them. After a long voyage they could often be persuaded that women and drink were desirable and the crimps undertook to supply both. After a few days of loose living and once more without funds they would be dumped aboard other ships at sailing time, and it was not uncommon for ships to be delayed until drink-sodden crews were in a fit state to undertake their duties. Without any advance of wages due to them, these men would frequently be destitute and be possessed of no more gear than the pitifully inadequate clothes they stood up in. In circumstances such as these it was not unknown for a shipmaster to give his own jacket to the man at the wheel to enable him to remain at his post in cold weather.

The Act of 1850 was no more than a move in the right direction, and throughout the second half of the 19th century further acts were passed which showed increasing concern for the safety and seaworthiness of ships and the well-being of their crews. These reforms did not come, of course, without effort on the part of farsighted men and prominent among the reformers of this period was Samuel Plimsoll, popularly known as 'the sailors' friend', who for many years directed much eloquence towards the passing of bills designed to safeguard seafarers. Although Plimsoll's propaganda methods were sometimes questionable, he was undoubtedly sincere, and the evil of 'coffin-ships' which he sought to end was no myth. On the other hand it must be pointed out that the reforms which Plimsoll adopted so enthusiastically as his own were first propounded by the shipowner James Hall. Not all shipowners were as black as Plimsoll painted them.

That it was high time some action was taken by the government is indicated by the fact that in the nine years ending in 1875 the number of British vessels lost, excluding fishing vessels,was 9,921. Many of these were colliers, small and often ill-found vessels which plied between the north-east coast and the Thames. Although seamen had the right to refuse to sail in any unseaworthy vessel, if they did so they sometimes ended up in gaol for refusing to obey lawful commands. Plimsoll's own Merchant Shipping Bill was pushed aside in 1875, but Disraeli's government saw fit to placate the public indignation he had aroused by introducing an Unseaworthy Ships Bill of their own. This stated that every ship registered after 1st January, 1876, should be marked withload lines 'not less than twelve inches in length and one inch in breadth painted longitudinally on each side amidships'. This was only a beginning to legislation which gradually extended government control over the marking of the load-line, the living space allocated to seafarers, the minimum quantities and qualities of the food he was to receive, and much else that was to improve the conditions under which the seaman serves. Nowadays Plimsoll's name is recalled every time the load line is referred to as the Plimsoll mark, though Londoners have been known so far to forget the past as to imagine, when seeing the familiar symbol below the Plimsoll Memorial on the Thames embankment, that this must be the founder of London Transport.

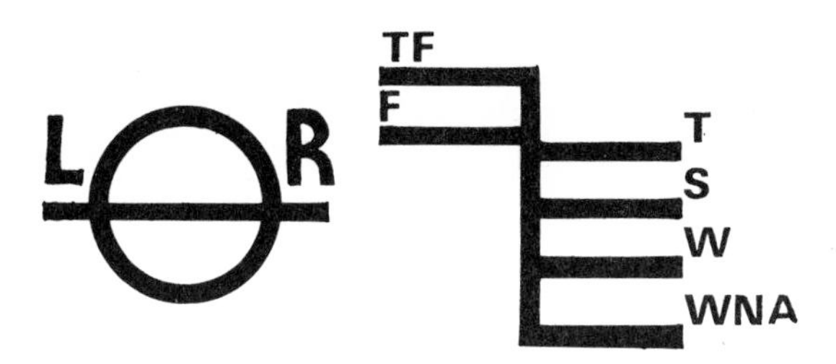

Fig 2 The modern load line or 'Plimsoll mark'
The deck line is a horizontal line marked amidships. Below it is the load line, its upper edge passing through the centre of the disc, which in this case is authorised by the Committee of Lloyd's Register (LR). This is the summer load line. Forward of the disc are horizontal lines which indicate the maximum depth to which the ship may be loaded in different circumstances and different seasons, namely: TF tropical fresh water load line; F fresh water load line; T tropical load line; S summer load line; W winter load line; WNA winter North Atlantic load line. Ships carrying timber are assigned an additional set of horizontal lines abaft the disc, the same lettering being prefixed by an 'L' (for lumber or timber).

A new era

It should not be thought that the Government alone tried to improve the conditions under which seafarers served. Jonas Hanway had founded the Marine Society in 1756 to help poor boys make a career at sea, and the Society established the first training ship in 1786, thus pioneering a method of training which was to last for more than 150 years. Missionary societies like The Missions to Seamen were prominent in fighting the crimping system and in establishing clubs and hotels which would serve the seaman well when he was away from home. The British Sailors' Society was founded in 1833, and the young clergyman, John Ashley, from whose work grew The Missions to Seamen, first began to visit the ships that thronged the Bristol Channel in 1835. The familiar Flying Angel flag was designed in 1856 when his work was first established on a national basis.

Seamen, too, began to help themselves. Indeed as early as the second half of the 18th century the seafarers of the north-east had formed local associations of various kinds, but it was Havelock Wilson, a seafarer from Sunderland, who first organised seamen on a national basis. Wilson founded his National Amalgamated Sailors' and Firemen's Union–now the National Union of Seamen–in July, 1887, though it was many years before it was thoroughly well established. Early attempts to promote solidarity by asking members to refuse to sail with non-union men landed Wilson in the law courts and began a series of legal actions which lasted for twenty-five years and sent him to gaol for six weeks in 1890. This was during the Bristol Channel strike when Wilson clashed with the newly formed Shipping Federation which represented the employers' interests. That strike was one of many which occurred in a period ending with the seamen's strike of 1911 and many times the union was near bankruptcy.

Indeed in1894, the year that witnessed the passing of the Merchant Shipping Act, an act which consolidated earlier legislation and which has remained the principal British act concerned with Merchant Navy affairs, the union did go into voluntary liquidation but only to rise again, phoenix-like, as the National Sailors' and Firemen's Union.

The First World War marked a great step forward in industrial relations at sea. It had been preceded in1911 by an official seamen's strike–the last until the strike of 1966–and it was followed in 1919 by the peacetime establishment of the National Maritime Board as a negotiating body for the representatives of shipowners and seafarers–a new piece of machinery by means of which wages and working conditions could be agreed without resort to violence, strike or lock-out.

It was perhaps also symptomatic of a new attitude to the welfare of seamen that, with the help of the Blue Funnel Line, Dr Albert Mansbridge succeeded in this same year in establishing the Seafarers Eduction Service, a society (now incorporated in The Marine Society) concerned to supply a library service to British merchant ships and to provide general education facilities for the benefit of British seafarers.

However, it was not all plain sailing from 1919 onwards. By this time, of course, the wind-driven ship was finished, despite the survival of a few of these vessels into the period between the two world wars. The mechanically propelled vessel, on the other hand, had become both the safest and the most economical means of transport and, unlike the sailing vessel, there was virtually no limit to its size except that dictated by the depth of water in the ports. Nevertheless, there was trouble in store. At the outbreak of the First World War Britain owned forty per cent of the world's shipping and carried half the world's trade, but she could not keep her engineering skill to herself. Stimulated by war, other nations began to build ships, and by 1921 there was little profit in shipping. The great slump had begun.

It was in this year that Captain W H Coombs resigned his post with the Chinese Maritime Customs to return home to establish The Navigators and General Insurance Company. The main purpose of 'The Navigators' was to insure Merchant Navy officers against the possible withdrawal of their certificates of competency, but from these beginnings, and in consequence of Coombs' inerest in officers' conditions of service, grew the Navigators and Engineer Officers Union, now the Merchant Navy and Airline Officers Association. This was not the first time that an attempt had been made to organise the officers of the Merchant Navy, for the work of the Mercantile Marine Service Association goes back to the middle years of the nineteenth century, those years in which compulsory examination had been introduced, but the work of Captain Coombs gave new life to the officers' organisations and led to considerable advances both in the status of officers and in their standard of living.

At the outbreak of the Second World War Britain's merchant fleet was still by far the largest in the world though, at 18 million tons gross it was one millions tons smaller than it had been in 1914, and as a proportion of the world fleet it had declined from 39 per cent to 26 per cent. It soon became apparent in wartime that Britain could not survive without its Merchant Navy, and the men of the Merchant Navy gave service which in terms of the proportionate sacrifice of human life exceeded any that was rendered by the Armed Forces of the United Kingdom. It has been estimated that, excluding Asians serving in British ships, the number of British merchant seamen serving at sea during the war years at no time much exceeded 145,000; nevertheless, 40,000 of these valiant men lost their lives, and British losses of merchant shipping exceeded 11 million tons.

Since the Second World War great progress has been made in improving still further the conditions under which seafarers serve. Stemming from a National

Maritime Board agreement, the Merchant Navy Establishment Scheme came into operation in 1947, replacing the wartime Merchant Navy Reserve Pool. Under this scheme a seafarer with the necessary qualifying service could be given a two-year contract, renewable for further periods. Since then, by negotiation with the shipowners on the national Maritime board, the seafarers' organisations have secured increases in wages and further improvements in working conditions which have at least matched what has been achieved in industry ashore. Through Government and industrial action, stimulated in some cases by International Labour Office conventions, new standards of safety, hygiene and medical care have been established, and most British shipowners have gone well beyond the Government's minimum standards in providing such amenities at sea as will compensate, in part at least, for the seafarer's inevitable separation from his family and the comforts of home life.

Ashore, the Merchant Navy Welfare Board was established in 1948 as the successor to a wartime Seamen's Welfare Board. This Board led the way in establishing new and high standards of accommodation in clubs and hotels for seafarers and, although most of these clubs and hotels are still run by societies which have been associated with such work for more than a century, the seafarer has long ceased to be the object of 'charity' which he was in days gone by.

A new revolution in both British and world shipping–greater than the change from sail to steam–may be dated from 1966, the year of a major seamen's strike, though its roots go back to the years immediately before this, being nourished by the growth of air transport, the closure of the Suez Canal and labour troubles in the docks. The Pearson and Rochdale reports on the shipping industry were symptomatic of new thinking, the former pointing the way to the Merchant Shipping Act of 1970, which adopted a new approach to the maintenance of discipline.

The facets of this shipping revolution are many. First, air transport has killed the passenger liner, the carriage of people by sea being mainly vestigial and in the form of holiday cruises and car ferries; this has greatly reduced the number of stewards in the Merchant Navy.

Second, ships generally have become fewer, faster and bigger, the growth in size being nowhere better illustrated than by tankers. In 1951 the term 'supertanker' was coined to describe a new large class of tanker of some 30,000 tons deadweight. In 1966 a 200,000 deadweight-ton tanker came into service and even bigger tankers are now afloat. Allied to this development has been the building of other specialised vessels like liquefied gas, chemical and ore carriers, ships which are more economic than their predecessors even though they do one leg of their voyage in ballast.

Third, container ships have increasingly replaced conventional cargo liners on major trade routes, a service to Australia being inaugurated in 1969 and since extended to other continents.

Fourth, the development of offshore gas and oil resources has led to a rapid growth in the number of rigs and of vessels of various shapes and sizes to service and move them.

Fifth and sixth have been the growth at sea of automation and the concomitant introduction of 'general purpose' crews to replace the old and hitherto sacrosanct division between seamen and greasers; this has further reduced the number of seafarers but increased their productivity and their standard of living.

One result of these changes, combined with an increase in world trade, was a rapid growth in the tonnage of the British Merchant Navy. After half a century in which the gross tonnage had varied (outside the war years) between 19 and 21 million tons it shot up to a peak of 33 million tons (51 million tons deadweight) in 1975, since which time there has been some decline.

A technological revolution in the Merchant Navy has necessitated advances in training methods and some change in the seaman. Three hundred years ago Edward Barlow ran away to sea and made something of his life there with little in the way of formal education. But Barlow was an exceptional man, a man with quite outstanding natural gifts who was also lucky to survive to tell his tale.

No young person runs away to sea now; but when anyone joins the modern Merchant Navy he or she does not require Barlow's luck or genius to make good. Down the centuries the sea has not changed. The conditions of the seafarer's life and his opportunities for advancement, on the other hand, have changed beyond all recognition. The modern seafarer needs to be more sophisticated, better educated and better able to stand on his own than the seaman of yesteryear. In the old days many seamen were orphans or came from broken homes, and many sought some substitute home in a ship. This would prove an unsound beginning to a sea career today, for the modern ship can prove a lonely place, and deep-sea ships spend little time in port. The modern seafarer needs to be self-reliant and self-disciplined and able to be happily alone at times.

Important Dates in Merchant Navy History
[c = circa or about]

BC

c.1500 Evidence of seafaring in British waters; Phoenicians trading with Egypt.

c.500 The Phoenician Himilco may have reached Brittany and seen Celtic skin boats.

c.320	The Greek Pytheas makes a voyage in northern waters.
55	Caesar defeats the Veneti seamen, who possess ships with leather sails, in the English Channel, and invades Britain.
AD	
c.519	St Brendan and other Irish seafarers venturing into the Atlantic; may have discovered Iceland.
793	Sack of Lindisfarne; Viking attacks on Britain begin.
896	Alfred the Great orders the building of large warships–the first English Navy.
1000	Leif Ericsson discovers North America.
1189	Third Crusade; Richard the Lionheart one of the leaders.
c.1194	The Judgments of Oléron.
1256	Conference of Baltic ports, first form of Hanseatic League.
1317	First official record of the Flanders galleys.
1344	Hakluyt's Voyages tell of English discovery of Madeira.
1374	Geoffrey Chaucer becomes Comptroller of the Customs and Subsidy of Wools with his office in the Custom House of the Port of London.
1433	Rounding of Cape Bojador, first achievement of Henry the Navigator, grandson of John of Gaunt.
1486	Bartholomew Diaz rounds the Cape of Good Hope.
1492	Columbus discovers the West Indies.
1497	John Cabot discovers North America.
1498	Vasco da Gama arrives in Calicut and discovers the sea route to India.
1499	Amerigo Vespucci charts part of the South American coast.
1508	First marine insurance in England.
1513	Balboa discovers the Pacific.
1514	Henry VIII incorporates Trinity House by Royal Charter.
1519	Magellan begins the first circumnavigation of the world.
1530	William Hawkins' first voyage to Africa and Brazil.
1542	First Portuguese reach Japan.
1545	First treatise on navigation published.
1562-8	John Hawkins' three slave-trading voyages to West Indies.
1576	Frobisher makes first attempt to find the North-West Passage.
1577-80	Drake's voyage round the world.
1588	Defeat of the Spanish Armada.
1600	First East India Company formed.
1620	The Pilgrim Fathers settle in North America.
1624	English driven out of the Spice Islands by the Dutch.
1651	Cromwell's Navigation Act, designed to harm Dutch trade.

1652 Foundation of Cape Colony by Dutch.
1660 Restoration of the monarchy; Charles II King; Board of Trade and Plantations established.
1667 Dutch fleet in the Medway.
1670 The Hudson's Bay Company formed.
1688 William of Orange lands; the first notice of Edward Lloyd's Coffee-House.
1696 William III founds Greenwich Hospital for sailors; *Lloyd's News* founded and soon fails.
1700 First dock opened in London; marine barometer invented.
1704 Gibraltar taken by the English.
1713 Monopoly of Spanish-American slave-trade granted to the English.
1720 The South Sea Bubble; the Royal Exchange Assurance Corporation and London Assurance granted charters.
1731 Sextant invented.
1734 *Lloyd's List* first published.
1735 Harrison invents marine chronometer.
1756 The Marine Society founded.
1760 Underwriters at Lloyd's form a Society to publish register of ships insured by them.
1767 First Nautical Almanac.
1768-76 Captain Cook's three voyages.
1772 Harrison's chronometer fulfils conditions laid down by the Board of Longitude and wins prize.
1773 The Boston Tea Party.
1786 First Registration of Shipping, London. The Marine Society establishes first training ship.
1787 Registration of Shipping throughout the Empire; first iron barge built.
1788 First settlement in Australia; Sydney founded.
1790 Lifeboats first used.
1798 River Police instituted in London.
1802 *Charlotte Dundas* steamship tried in Scotland and tows barges; West India Docks opened in London.
1805 Nelson's victory at Trafalgar.
1812 *Comet* completed on the Clyde, recognised as the first practical steamship.
1813 First notice of an iron cable being part of ship's equipment in *Lloyd's Register*.
1815 Battle of Waterloo, end of the Napoleonic Wars; first steamship on the Thames.

1818 *Savannah*, auxiliary powered sailing vessel, crosses the Atlantic.
1822 First steamship registered by Lloyd's.
1824 Foundation of the General Steam Navigation Company and the Royal National Life-boat Institution.
1832 Electric telegraph invented.
1833 Trade with India thrown open.
1836 Committee set up to inquire into the cause of wrecks.
1837 The P&O Company founded; first iron ship registered by Lloyd's.
1838 *Great Western* and *Sirius* cross the Atlantic, the *Great Western* beginning the first regular service which took 17 days; the screw propeller introduced.
1839 Cunard Company founded as British and North American Royal Mail Steam Packet Co.
1840 Penny Post; first Cunard steamer, *Britannia*, sailed.
1847 Gold discovered in California.
1848 North-West Passage discovered.
1849 Navigation Laws repealed.
1850 Mercantile Marine Act; examination of masters and mates begins.
1851 First submarine telegraph.
1853 Admiral Perry forces trade with Japan.
1854 Merchant Shipping Act–548 sections.
1855 Meteorological Office established.
1857 Mercentile Marine Service Association founded; International Code of Signals established.
1858 *Great Eastern* launched, a commercial failure but ultimately a successful cable ship; first message by Atlantic cable, not permanently successful until 1866.
1859 Royal Naval Reserve authorised.
1861 Beginning of the American Civil War; decline of American shipping; storm warnings first issued.
1862 International Rule of the Road at Sea settled; first examination of marine engineers.
1863 Twin-screws used.
1865 End of the American Civil War; foundation of the Ocean Steam Ship Company, known as the Blue Funnel Line.
1866 Successful Atlantic cable laid by *Great Eastern*.
1869 Suez Canal opened; *Cutty Sark* launched.
1870 Ice-breaking vessel first employed.
1871 Lloyd's incorporated.
1872 Daily weather-charts first issued.
1876 First Load Line Act; until 1890 owners able to place mark where they pleased.

1878 The Chamber of Shipping of the United Kingdom formed.
1880 First shipments of frozen mutton arrive in England from Australia.
1881 ss *Aberdeen* built with triple-expansion engines.
1884 Parsons built first steam turbine engine.
1886 *Gluckauf* first tank steamer built.
1887 National Amalgamated Sailors' and Firemen's Union (now the National Union of Seamen) founded by Havelock Wilson.
1890 Shipping Federation (now incorporated within the General Council of British Shipping) founded.
1894 Merchant Shipping Act passed, consolidating former Acts–748 sections; Manchester Ship Canal opened; *Turbinia*, first turbine steamer, launched on the Tyne.
1895 Kiel Ship Canal opened.
1900 Wireless telegraphy adopted by the Admiralty.
1901 First permanent wireless installation at sea in *Lucania*.
1903 Dr Diesel's first successful marine engine fitted to barge.
1904 Panama Canal concession acquired by United States; steam turbines adopted by Cunard.
1908 Formation of the Port of London Authority.
1910 Board of Trade Committee on sight tests.
1911 Gyroscopic compass invented.
1912 *Titanic* disaster, April 15th.
1914 Panama Canal opened.
1914-18 First World War–submarine warfare.
1919 Seafarers Education Service founded.
1922 Introduction of the term Merchant Navy; hitherto the expressions Mercantile Marine and Merchant Service were commonly used.
1926 Honourable Company of Master Mariners founded.
1928 The title of 'Master of the Merchant Navy and Fishing Fleets' created by King George V, who conferred it upon Edward Prince of Wales (later Duke of Windsor). Pacific flown.
1935 Navigators and Engineer Officers Union founded by Captain W H Coombs; now the Merchant Navy and Airline Officers Association.
1936 *Queen Mary*, maiden voyage.
1939-45 Second World War; at least 40,000 British merchant seamen lost their lives, proportionally more than in any of the fighting services.
1940 *Queen Elizabeth*, maiden voyage.
1944 Publication of the International Seafarers' Charter, symbolic of a new attitude to seafarers' conditions.

1946 The Seattle Conference: the conventions, recommendations and resolutions adopted set the pattern for industrial agreements in many maritime countries.
1952 Able seamen required to have a certificate.
1955 Merger of Navigators and Engineer Officers Union and Marine Engineers Association to form Merchant Navy and Airline Officers Association.
1958 Passengers carried across the Atlantic by air first exceeded passengers carried by sea.
1961 Atomic-powered merchant ship *Savannah* launched.
1965 Containerisation introduced on the North Atlantic by Sea-Land.
1966 The first 200,000dwt tanker entered service. UK seamen's strike.
1970 New Merchant Shipping Act.
1972 The Nautical Institute founded.
1975 General Council of British Shipping formed from merger of the Chamber of Shipping and the British Shipping Federation.
1977 New Rule of the Road at sea adopted.
1979 New Code of Conduct for British seafarers adopted.

2 British Shipping Today

there is no thrill
Like stepping ashore in a new country
With a clean shirt and with pound-notes
in your pocket.
Charles Causley (from *Union Street*)

All young people want to see the world and even today, when ships make speedy turn-rounds, they are better able to see it in the Merchant Navy than in any other profession. Because the Merchant Navy has been described as the 'fourth arm of defence', some of those ashore imagine its organisation is similar to that of the Royal Navy, but this is not so. The merchant seafarer's is essentially a civilian occupation. Although he may wear uniform at sea, he rarely wears it ashore; and such discipline as he endures at sea is a discipline that is largely imposed upon the ship by the sea itself.

In the Merchant Navy there are many different companies and many different jobs, but all the careers are open to the talents and the Merchant Navy is the most democratic of professions. It can also be a fascinating one. However old and however experienced the seafarer, the land that rises above the horizon retains its magic; and the moods of the sea and the climates of the world are such that there is always something to look forward to even on those occasions when the present is not immediately enjoyable.

Of course, life in the Merchant Navy is not all honey. For some the sweet taste of their honeymoon period lasts but a short time, particularly if the seafarer has no inner resources; even for others the pull of home and wives is a powerful pull. Nevertheless, the man who regrets his time at sea in the Merchant Navy is a rare man. For those who are temperamentally suited to a Merchant Navy career, the rewards, whether financial or of other kinds, measure up well to those in alternative professions.

Nowadays the Merchant Navy is an industry of modest size. The population of the United Kingdom is 55,000,000 and of this number rather less than one-half– 26,000,000–go to work. Of these workers a mere 70,000 are employed at sea in the Merchant Navy, excluding some 11,500 Commonwealth seafarers whose homes are not in the United Kingdom. This is half the number employed a generation ago and not much more than a quarter of those employed at the beginning of the century. Indeed today there are fewer merchant seamen in the United Kingdom then there are civil servants in the Inland Revenue. In addition to those employed at sea, British shipping companies employ about 20,000 people in their company offices.

Despite its modest work force the Merchant Navy is vital to Britain's continued existence. British ships carry nearly one-half of the country's imports and exports, and the net contribution to the United Kingdom balance of payments of UK ships is more than £1,000 million. This sum represents receipts from abroad, less payments made abroad for bunkers and port and cargo-handling charges. A large part of these export earnings come from trade between overseas countries, the so-called cross-trades. However, for the first time in perhaps 200 years, the United Kingdom moved into deficit on its sea transport account in 1978. In other words, in that year, less was earned by British shipping than was paid out to foreign shipping. This has important defence as well as economic significance. Unlike many other nations, which could still exist if every ship were sunk without trace, Britain would starve within weeks if merchant ships did not arrive regularly to unload their cargoes. The Merchant Navy is of vital concern not merely to those whose livelihood is directly related to it; it is of vital concern to every inhabitant of the United Kingdom. Unfortunately, all too many people are unaware that this is so.

Merchant shipping is one of the most capital intensive of all industries. A new 15,000 deadweight-ton general cargo ship costs something like £8 million, a 100,000 deadweight-ton tanker costs rather more than £30 million and a 32,000 deadweight-ton container ship costs upwards of £40 million. Each of these ships might be run by a crew of 30.

Allowing for the age of the ships which constitute it, the current (1980) value of the British merchant fleet is of the order of £11,000 million. On average each merchant seafarer is working with £150,000 of capital equipment, and each of those aboard a container ship is working with capital equipment valued at more than £1 million.

UK FLEET, TYPES OF SHIP	NUMBER OF SHIPS	TONNAGE GROSS TONS	AVERAGE SIZE GROSS TONS
Tankers and gas carriers	510	14,620,859	28,688
Other bulk carriers	217	6,627,629	30,542
Container ships	85	1,772,465	20,852
Dry cargo ships	859	3,275,411	3,813
Ferries and passenger vessels	167	641,947	3,844
Supply ships and tenders	189	278,603	1,474
Dredgers	152	216,734	1,426
Tugs	345	121,329	352
Fishing vessels	507	170,100	336
Miscellaneous	180	226, 265	1,257
Total	3,211	27,951,342	(8,705)

Fig 3 UK fleet: types of ship

Types of ships

The British merchant fleet is made up of some 3,200 steamships and motorships, all of them currently powered by fuel oil. This is little more than half the number of ships sailing under the red ensign at the end of World War II, though the ships have increased in size and the total tonnage is higher. The peak tonnage figure, in 1975, was 33 million gross tons. This has since fallen to 27 million gross tons and represents no more than 6 per cent of the world fleet of 413 million gross tons. This is a dramatically smaller proportion of the world fleet than it was a generation or two ago.

Nowadays it is also customary to express these figures in terms of deadweight tonnage for reasons shortly to be explained and, since deadweight tons have been used above and are given below for company fleet sizes, it can be noted here that the UK fleet of 27 million gross tons is also of 40 million deadweight tons and the world fleet of 413 million gross tons is of 680 million deadweight tons.

Nearly one-half of the 3,200 ships in the UK fleet consists of small, non-trading vessels–fishing vessels, tugs, supply ships and tenders, dredgers, research ships and others. Despite their large number these account for only 6 per cent of the tonnage. The remaining 1,671 trading ships, which account for

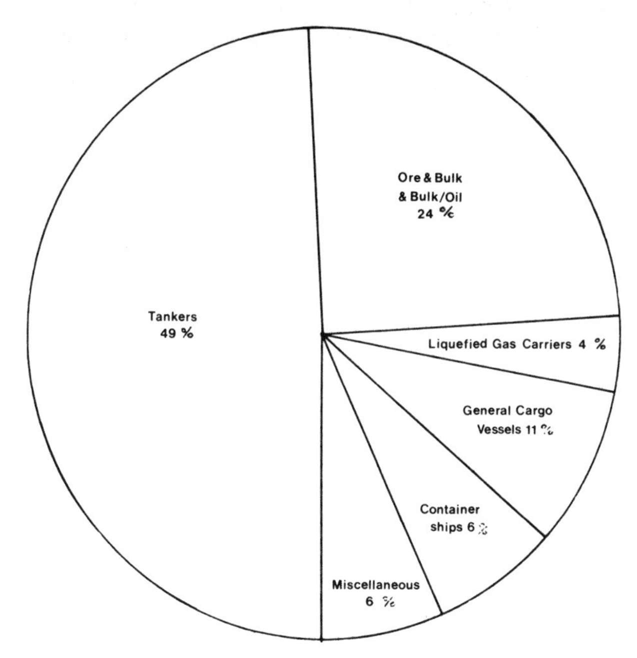

Fig 4 Composition of the British merchant fleet (by gross tonnage)

94 per cent of the total tonnage, are of many different types engaged in many different trades, the main types and the main trades being indicated in Figure 4.

At least 25 per cent of the UK fleet is owned by foreign companies, such companies as Mobil, Texaco, CP, Esso and Buries Markes. The British-owned fleet does not much exceed 20 million gross tons or 30 million deadweight tons and is only some 5 per cent of the world shipping total. Seventy years ago this figure was in excess of 40 per cent.

Since the end of the second world war, and particularly since 1965, a dramatic change has taken place in the nature of shipping. Nowadays *tankers* comprise almost exactly one-half of the British merchant fleet as measured by gross tonnage, and some 43 per cent of the world fleet of merchant ships. Much of Britain's tanker tonnage belongs to the oil companies, notably Shell, BP, Mobil, Texaco and Esso, but some other companies own tankers, chartering or hiring them to the oil companies for the carriage of their products. Before the war British tanker tonnage was negligible and even 15 years ago tankers made up only one-third of the fleet.

The largest tankers–now more than 200,000 deadweight tons–often operate between the countries of supply, those countries bordering upon the Arabian Gulf and the Caribbean Sea, for example, and the major terminals in the industrialised countries. These are the VLCCs (very large crude carriers) and ULCCs (ultra large crude carriers). The largest of these ships are not much short of a quarter of a mile long.

Smaller tankers or products carriers, perhaps of 30,000 deadweight tons, are sent to maintain supplies of refined oils of different kinds wherever these may be required. They are frequently operated like tramp steamers. Other tankers of similar size may be used to lighten VLCCs and ULCCs where the depth of water in a port is too shallow to allow the big tankers to enter the port fully loaded. There are also tankers specially designed to carry chemicals of various kinds.

Other specialised vessels, akin in many ways to tankers, include a growing fleet of ore carriers built to meet the iron ore requirements of the steel industry. Similar bulk carriers have been built for other trades–for the movement of such other ores as bauxite, for the movement of coal and grain, and even for the sugar trade. There are also vessels which can be used to carry oil, iron ore or other bulk cargoes (*OBO ships*), as the needs of trade require. The sizes of such ships normally range from 30,000 to 140,000 deadweight tons. They have increased greatly as a proportion of the UK fleet in the past 15 years and now comprise one-quarter of the gross tonnage.

Significant enough nowadays to warrant a category of their own are the liquefied natural and petroleum gas carriers (*LNGs* and *LPGs*), for these highly sophisticated vessels constitute 4 per cent of the present-day fleet. They are likely to be about 50,000 deadweight tons.

All the ships mentioned so far have one thing in common: they normally travel one way in ballast or carrying no cargo.

The tonnage of *general cargo vessels*, taken as a whole, is now a mere 11 per cent of the UK fleet. Fifteen years ago it was proportionately four times this amount. These ships mostly carry mixed cargoes of mainly dry goods or manufactures and aim to fill their holds with profitable parcels of cargo whatever the direction of their voyage. Some of them have been designed to carry refrigerated cargoes of meat and dairy produce or cooled cargoes of fruit, while others again are fitted with tanks for the carriage of vegetable oils. Some can carry refrigerated cargo on one leg of a voyage and cars on another. At least one has been specially designed to carry live animals from Australia to Singapore. These ocean-going vessels are mostly between 6,000 and 15,000 gross tons (9,000–18,000 deadweight tons) with crews numbering between 30 and 40.

If general cargo vessels operate on a regular service between particular ports in general accordance with a previously advertised schedule they are known as *liners*. If they are not operated on any fixed route but are available for hire at the freight rates prevailing in the world shipping markets, sailing to where the hirer or charterer wishes the ships to go and where there are cargoes to be lifted, they are known as *tramps, trampers* or *tramp steamers*. Tramps may be engaged in the carriage of such bulk cargoes as grain, coal, timber and ores, but much of this trade has fallen away with the building of the specialised vessels described above. The modern tramp, however, is a fine and speedy vessel capable of being put to a variety of uses and, on occasion, tramps are hired by liner companies for temporary incorporation in a liner service.

Tankers, bulk-carriers and dry-cargo vessels are, of course, far more typical of the Merchant Navy than are the famous passenger liners like *Queen Elizabeth 2* which in the past have captured the public imagination and which employ crews numbering several hundred men and women. The profits of the traditional passenger liner have been eroded by the development of the jet aircraft and the number of passenger liners has decreased rapidly. Those that still exist are largely operated as *cruise-ships*, and nowadays such vessels are built with cruising principally in mind. The few general cargo vessels which at one time carried a dozen passengers have also disappeared, for the provision of this type of passenger accommodation has become increasingly uneconomic, the labour costs being too high for the return yielded.

In recent years the *container ship*, which normally runs to a strict liner schedule, has been developed to carry all cargo which can be packed conveniently into containers, the large boxes (normally 20 × 10 × 10 feet) often seen ashore being transported by long vehicles. Container ships range from 20,000 to 50,000 deadweight tons, but their capacity is normally stated in terms of the number of standard containers they can carry. The capacity of

Cardigan Bay, for example, is 2,450 teus (or 20-foot equivalent units). Containers can be as much as 40 feet long. The advantage of container ships lies in their speedy turn-round: to load and unload container ships takes only a few hours, whereas to unload a dry-cargo vessel can take weeks. Container ships have taken much of the trade of the traditional cargo liner and more and more cargo vessels are being adapted or built to carry some containers. In this way they can provide a 'feeder' service to and from ports not on container ship routes.

Among the other specialised vessels that make up a part of the Merchant Navy are car ferries, oil-rig supply vessels, cable ships (for the laying and repairing of submarine telegraph and telephone cables), weather ships, Royal Fleet Auxiliary vessels, and ocean-going tugs and salvage craft. Oil-rigs in the sea are a growing feature of the maritime scene and special vessels have been developed to supply and move them.

Cutting across this division of ships into tankers, bulkers, OBOs, gas carriers, general cargo vessels, cruise-ships, container ships and other specialised vessels is the division of ships into those engaged in the deepsea or oceangoing trades, those engaged in the home or short-sea trades to continental Europe, and those engaged in the coastal trade around the British Isles. It is noteworthy that, unlike the United States and many other countries, the United Kingdom does not reserve its coastal trade for its own ships only and in this coastal trade, as on the high seas, British ships are subject to foreign competition.

Tonnage

From earliest times it has been necessary to assess the size of ships and, as far as English ships are concerned, the first method known was that used in the Bordeaux wine trade. A ship of a certain length, breadth and depth was found to carry a certain number of barrels of wine called–unfortunately for the purposes of clarity–tuns. The number of tuns was found to be about one tun for every 100 cubic feet of this block measurement. The tun held 252 gallons and, the gallon measure in use in the 15th century being rather different from the imperial, the weight of a tun of wine was about a ton. The tun thus served for both weight and measurement.

Nowadays, in describing ships, the word 'ton' is used in a number of different senses. Until recently the statistics of merchant ships were normally given in gross tons (or tons gross)–the ton directly related to the 15th century tun–except in the case of tankers and other bulk carriers where it was common to give the deadweight tonnage. Because these latter vessels now account for about three-quarters of the tonnage afloat it is becoming increasingly common to present general statistics in terms of deadweight tonnage. There is no fixed relationship between the two and accurate conversion is not always possible or even meaningful. Both deadweight and gross tonnages are used in the text and it is necessary to observe which are used in each case.

TONNAGE	IS EQUAL TO	IS USED FOR
1 deadweight ton	1 ton weight of cargo, fuel and water carried	Tankers and bulk carriers and some statistics
1 gross ton	100 cubic feet of permanently enclosed space	Purposes of a ship's registration, calculating pilotage charges and dry-dock dues, and for general statistics
1 net ton	1 gross ton minus the cubic capacity of non-earning spaces	Volume of earning space for port and canal dues and for statistics of entrances and clearances of ships at port
1 displacement ton	1 ton weight of water displaced when ship is afloat	Calculating stability and shipbreaking values
1 gross ton	roughly 1.5 deadweight tons	

Fig 5 Tonnage

Deadweight tonnage (dwt) is the actual weight in tons of cargo, fuel, water, passengers and crew that a ship can carry when down to her loadline or Plimsoll mark. In other words it is the difference between the number of tons of water a vessel displaces when unloaded or'light' and the number of tons it displaces when submerged to the loadline. Broadly speaking, a 200,000-ton deadweight tanker will carry 200,000 tons of oil, and deadweight tonnage is a ship's cargo-carrying capacity.

Gross tonnage (grt or gross registered tonnage) is a space measurement, a measurement of ship size, whereby the sum of all the closed-in spaces below the upper deck, including machinery space, crew decks and other spaces not available for carriage, as well as carriage space, plus spaces above the upper deck strictly necessary for carriage, is expressed in units of 100 cubic feet. One gross ton is equal to 100 cubic feet of permanently enclosed space. Gross tonnage is used for the purposes of a ship's registration, in the calculation of pilotage charges and dry-dock dues, and for universal statistics. It relates neither to the weight nor to the earning power of a ship, but it is the only tonnage applicable to all types of ship and the only legal form of measurement. IMCO (IMO) dues are estimated from gross tonnage.

Net tonnage is gross tonnage minus the cubic capacity of such non-earning spaces as the engine-room, fuel stores and crew accommodation, and is a measure of the volume of space available for earning. It tells one nothing about the weight of cargo carried since a ton of plastic flowers–a cargo sometimes carried from Hong Kong–will take up far more space than a ton of iron ore. The net tonnage is normally used in calculating the liability of ships to canal and port dues and in compiling statistics of entrances and clearances of ships at ports.

Displacement tonnage is the weight of water displaced by a ship when she is afloat. 'Displacement light' is the weight of a vessel without stores,bunker fuel or cargo. 'Displacement loaded' is the weight of a vessel with these extras taken into consideration. Displacement tonnage is used for measuring fighting ships and, in the Merchant Navy, for drydock stability calculations. It is also used for estimating the value of a ship when she goes to the shipbreakers.

It will be noted from what has been said above that both deadweight tonnage and net tonnage can be used to estimate earning capacity but, since one relates to weight carried and the other to space available, there is no direct relationship between them. Nor is there any way of converting gross tonnage accurately into deadweight tonnage. As a rough and ready conversion factor, however, one gross ton may be regarded as equivalent to 1.5 deadweight tons.

Nowadays the Certificate of Survey and British Tonnage Certificates have to show the gross and net register tonnages in both tons of 100 cubic feet and in the form of cubic metres. Cubic metres are obtained by multiplying tons by 2.83.

Company organisation

It is difficult to generalise about the organisation of a shipping company since so much depends upon the size of the company and the nature of its business. The business of many groups today includes much beside shipping.

In the one-ship tramp company of days gone by all that was necessary was to keep the ship on the move and to see that it was adequately manned and stored. With contracts for the carriage of cargo being arranged through the Baltic Exchange, no more than a marine-cum-engineers department plus a victualling-cum-accounts department were required at the shipping company office. The organisation of the liner company operating a fleet of ships was more complicated. The two departments appropriate to the tramp company usually became four, with more staff in each, and to these would be added new departments designed to deal with the complexities of general cargo and the carriage of passengers. Few companies now, however, are concerned with the carriage of passengers.

Whatever the fleet of ships, the directors will normally control, in one form or another: (a) a finance department; (b) a trade department; (c) a fleet department; and (d) a development department. The finance department will have overall control of the expenditure of money and be responsible for the accounts. The trade department will deal with the shippers of cargo and, where passengers are carried, with travel agents; it will be concerned with freight rates and liner conferences and with the handling of cargo; and it will generally try to maintain and increase the company's business. The fleet department will be concerned with the maintenance and storing of the ships and with the recruitment, training and welfare of the ships' companies or crews. The development department will be planning for the future, deciding how the fleet is to be developed, when ships are to be replaced and by what, and how the work on board those ships is to be carried out.

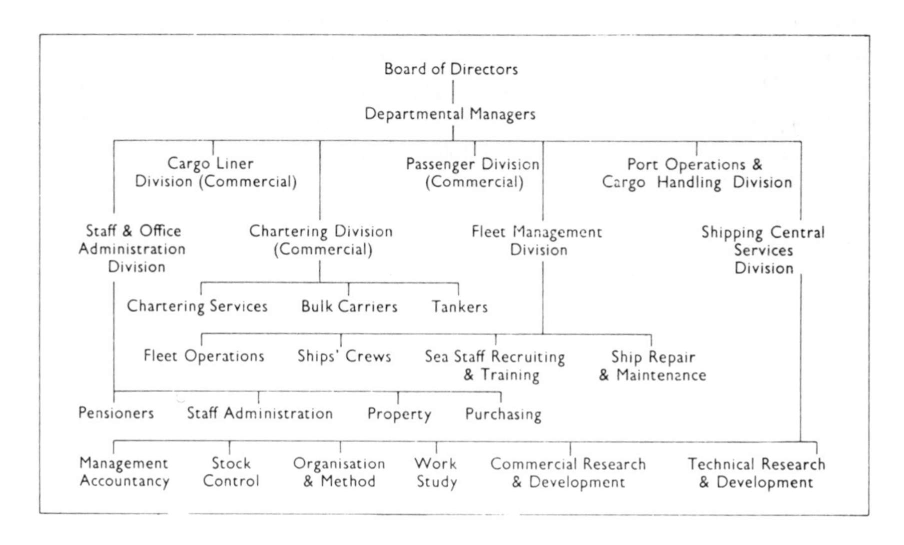

Fig 6 The structural organisation of one shipping group.

One possible structural organisation–that of a large and diversified group–is illustrated schematically and this diagram indicates how complex such organisation can become. Three trade or commercial departments exist here, one dealing with passengers, one with general cargo, and one with bulk carriers of all descriptions plus those vessels which are hired or chartered from other owners. A further department deals with port operations and the handling of cargo. Two more departments deal, respectively, with shore staff and sea staff, the former having office property under its control and the latter looking after floating property–ships–as well as the recruitment, training and welfare of seafarers. Lastly, a shipping central services division is concerned with all the business of planning the fleet and the work that is carried out by it, both now and in the future.

Principal shipping companies

Leaving on one side those small companies which operate tugs and the companies which are engaged in the fishing industry, British shipping is in the hands of just over 100 companies–no more than one-third of the number of companies twenty years ago. Fifty-six of these companies are listed below. They own well over 90 per cent of the total tonnage, and above 75 per cent of the number of trading vessels.

Since ships are being sold, scrapped and built all the time, and trades are changed to meet changing conditions, these figures can only give a picture at a particular instant of time–summer 1980. It must also be remembered that it is not nearly so easy as it used to be to classify shipping companies, and shipping becomes an increasingly international business. Here the companies have been listed in order of the deadweight tonnage owned and managed. This tends to give undue importance to the tanker operators, and to the 'managers' as distinct from the 'owners'. A cargo liner will cost twice as much per ton to build as a tanker and, though many times smaller in terms of deadweight tonnage, it may well carry a larger crew. Cunard operates as many ships as BP, but the total tonnage of the fleet is very much smaller, and much smaller proportionately than the relative number of seafarers employed. The figures given do not therefore indicate accurately a company's capital investment, a figure which is also dependent in part upon the age of the fleet; nor do they indicate accurately the company's significance as an employer of seafarers. If one is concerned principally with British seafarers, still more reservations must be made because many companies employ seafarers who live outside the United Kingdom. On the other hand, many foreign and Commonwealth shipping companies employ British officers.

Some fleets have changed greatly in recent years, and not all of the companies listed are British-owned.

Shell

Shell Tankers (UK) Limited, Shell Centre, London SE1 7PQ, is the company which owns and manages those ships of the Royal Dutch/Shell Group Fleet which are operated under the British flag. The company was founded in 1897 and trades world-wide. The 52 tankers, LNG and ore carriers operated total 6,415,000 tons deadweight. *Opalia*, uniquely among tankers, carries 28 deck cadets. Additionally, a few ships are managed for other companies.

Fig 7 Ships' names

Ships' names are not always what they used to be. In consequence of mergers and amalgamations, series of names which were once well known have either disappeared or become less than consistent. Most of the British series which remain are listed here.

ACT (A)	*ACT 1*, *2*, etc.
Bank Line (Andrew Weir)	Names end *bank*, eg *Firbank*
Ben Line	Many begin *Ben*, eg *Benvatta*
Bibby Line	After English counties, eg *Staffordshire*, except Dart Atlantic chartered to Dart Containerline.
Blue Star (Vestey)	Names end *Star*, eg *Africa Star*
B & C	Dry cargo liners have old Clan Line names beginning *Clan* and the bulk carriers perpetuate King Line names such as *King William*. The products tankers bear names beginning *Scottish* and the refrigerated ships now have names ending *Universal* as they are members of the Universal Reefers consortium.
Blue Funnel Bulkships (Ocean)	Ships named after Homeric characters, in keeping with the company's earliest traditions, eg *Ajax*
BP	Names begin British, eg *British Purpose*.
Buries Markes	Original Argentine connections indicated by names which mostly begin *La*, eg *La Selva*, although managed ships may have other names.
Cairn Line (Furness Withy)	Prefixed *Cairn*, eg *Cairnock*.
CP Ships	Names of the container vessels begin with the prefix *CP*, eg *CP Hunter*.
Cunard	Fruit carriers keep traditional names ending *ia*, eg *Alaunia*. Tankers begin *L*, eg *Lucerna*.

Denholm	Denholm Line steamers end *park*, eg *Wellpark*.
Elder Dempster (Ocean)	Mainly named after places in West Africa.
Ellerman	Names begin *City of* eg *City of Plymouth*.
Esso	Names begin *Esso*, eg *Esso Demetia*.
Everard	Named after members of family, eg *Ethel Everard* or end *ty*, eg *City*, *Commodity*.
Fyffes	Names feature rivers, bays, capes and other geographical features mainly in South America.
Harrison Line	Generally descriptive of classes of people, eg *Warrior*, *Astronomer*, etc.
Hogarth (SSM)	Names begin *Baron*, eg *Baron Murray*.
LOF	Names largely begin *London*, eg *London Baron*.
Jebsens (UK)	All names end *nes*, eg *Clydnes*.
Lowland Tankers (BP)	Names begin *Border*.
Lyle (SSM)	Begin *Cape*, eg *Cape Ortegal*.
Manchester Liners (Furness Withy)	Names begin *Manchester*, eg *Manchester Zeal*.
Mobil	Names begin Mobil, eg *Mobil Pinnacle*, but names associated with North American Indian chiefs are used for the North Sea tankers.
OCL	All names incorporate *Bay*, eg *Botany Bay*.
Offshore Marine (Cunard)	All names comprise two words, the second being *Shore*, eg *Mercia Shore*.
Palm Line	Names end *Palm*, eg *Africa Palm*.
Panocean-Anco	Prefixed *Anco*, eg *Anco Enterprise*.

(fig 7)

P&O	No standard naming system for the whole group but dry-cargo ships have names beginning *Strath*, eg *Stratheden*; most reefers have *Wild* birds' names, eg, *Wild Auk*; gas carriers have names in *Ga-a*, eg *Gazana*.
Port Line (Cunard)	Names begin *Port*, eg *Port Caroline*.
Prince Line (Furness Withy)	Names end *Prince*, eg *Crown Prince*.
Reardon Smith	Names end *City*, eg *Welsh City*.
Rowbotham	Names end *man*, eg *Helmsman*.
Salén UK	Bulk-carrier names end *Wasa*.
Shell	Latin names of sea-shells, eg *Labiosa*, *Opalia*.
Silver Line	Names begin *Silver*, eg *Silvereagle*, or end *Bridge*, eg *Erskine Bridge* if part of Seabridge. Vessels under Alva Shipholdings begin with *Al*, eg *Alvenas*, *Algol*.
Stephenson Clarke	Named after Sussex towns or precious stones.
Texaco	Names begin *Texaco*, eg *Texaco London*.
Turnbull Scott	Company's own ships have the suffix *gate*, eg *Baxtergate*.
United Baltic (Andrew Weir)	Begin *Baltic*, eg *Baltic Valiant*.

(fig 7)

Denholm

The Denholm Group whose head office is at 120 St Vincent Street, Glasgow G2 5EW, manages 85 ships totalling 6,000,000 tons deadweight, but owns only a few of them. Denholm Line Steamers was first registered in 1909. Now the company incorporates Denholm Maclay Company Limited, Inter City House, 80 Oswald Street, Glasgow G1 4PX, which in turn incorporates Triport Ferries (Management) Limited, and there are many other companies in the Group. Denholm is one of the biggest ship management companies in the world, its fleets including container ships, bulk carriers, tankers, chemical tankers, OBO's, reefers and ro-ros. Trade routes are world-wide. *Wellpark* is operated as a cadet ship. Some of the ships do not operate under the British flag.

BP

BP Tanker Company Limited, Britannic House, Moor Lane, London EC2Y 9BR, was first registered in 1909 as the Anglo-Persian Oil Company Limited. The company includes BP Thames Tanker Company, BP Tyne Tanker Company, Clyde Charter Company, Lowland Tanker Company, Tanker Charter Company and BP Medway Tanker Company. BP Tanker Company also have an interest in the Irano-British Ship Service Company Limited, which is a joint shipping venture with the National Iranian Tanker Company. The 58 tankers operated total 5,265,000 tons deadweight. The company is owned by the British Petroleum Company Limited which also owns drilling rigs and support vessels.

Mobil

Mobil Shipping Company Limited, Mobil House, 54-60 Victoria Street, London SW1E 6QB, a fully owned subsidiary of Mobil Corporation of the USA, manages 35 tankers of Mobil's international fleet totalling some 4,400,000 tons deadweight. Vessels range in size from 30,000 deadweight-ton product carriers to VLCCs engaged in world-wide trading, but two tankers are exclusively employed in Mobil's North Sea oil production.

P&O

P&O (in full, The Peninsular & Oriental Steam Navigation Company), Beaufort House, St Botolph Street, London EC3A 7DX, is a large multi-rôle transport Group. Its chief shipping operations are P&O Bulk Shipping, P&O Cruises, P&O Ferries, P&O Strath Services and Australian Offshore Services (part of P&O Australia Limited, 55 Hunter Street, Sydney). They cover most aspects of international trade, and the 96 ships of 2,395,395 tons deadweight owned or leased by the P&O Group include 17 general cargo ships, 15 refrigerated cargo ships, 11 passenger ferries, 9 cargo ferries, 9 liquefied petroleum gas carriers, 7 cruise ships, 7 offshore supply vessels, 4 tankers, 4 combination carriers, product and chemical tankers, tugs, hydrofoils, container ships, a bulk carrier and a passenger/cargo liner. P&O is associated with a number of joint shipping operations, notable Anglo Nordic Shipping, Associated Bulk Carriers, Lauritzen-Peninsular Reefers, LNG Carriers, Mundogas, North Sea Ferries, Overseas Containers (OCL) and Panocean. Incorporated by Royal

Charter in 1840, P&O grew up in the years that followed the abolition of the East India Company's trade monopoly, and it was on the mail routes to India, the Far East and Australia that P&O's fortunes were founded. Beginning in 1910 a group of subsidiary shipping companies was taken over, many of them widely known in their own right, including British India Steam Navigation Company, New Zealand Shipping Company, Orient Line, General Steam, Strick Line and the Hain and Nourse companies. A major reorganisation in 1971 brought these concerns' different shipping operations together into the present divisional structure. Funnels vary: bulk and cargo vessels have blue funnels with white 'P&O' logo; most ferries' funnels are blue with the P&O flag symbol though not all freight ferries carry the flag; passenger ship funnels are buff (*Canberra, Oriana, Sea Princess*), black with white bands (*Dwarka, Uganda*) or white with a blue-and-green 'Princess' symbol (*Island Princess, Pacific Princess, Sun Princess*).

Silver Line

Silver Line Limited, 7 Rolls Buildings, Fetter Lane, London EC4A 1BA (Silver Line/Navcot), owns and manages a fleet of 46 bulk carriers, chemical tankers and other vessels totalling some 2,500,000 tons deadweight and operating world-wide, some of them in the Seabridge consortium. The company is part of the Vlasov Group.

CP Ships

CP Ships, 50 Finsbury Square, London EC2A 1DD, is the shipping division of the Canadian Pacific Group and owns and operates 41 vessels including VLCCs, product and chemical carriers, geared and gearless bulk carriers and container ships totalling 2,488,241 tons deadweight.

Esso

Esso Petroleum Company Limited, Victoria Street, London SW1E 5JW, is the British flag Esso fleet, part of the American Exxon Group which owns some 15,500,000 tons deadweight of tankers. The British company consists of 29 tankers totalling 2,427,000 tons deadweight, and they carry crude oil or oil products world-wide.

Texaco

Texaco Overseas Tankship Limited, Mercury House, 195 Knightsbridge Green, London SW7 1RU, is part of the Texaco Group of Companies marketing petroleum products world-wide. It owns 20 British registered tankers and manages 2 more, the ships together totalling 2,297,293 tons deadweight. The ships carry crude oil and oil products world-wide.

Ocean

Ocean Transport & Trading Limited, India Buildings, Water Street, Liverpool L2 0RB, operates 44 ships totalling about 2,000,000 deadweight tons (1,157,698 gross tons). Alfred Holt, together with his brother Philip, founded the Ocean Steam Ship Company in 1865 for the purpose of trading to China. In 1902 it became a limited company and in the same year the China Mutual Steam Navigation Company was acquired. In 1935 Glen Line and in 1965 Elder Dempster Lines joined the Ocean Group. In 1973 the Ocean Steam Ship Company was renamed Ocean Transport & Trading. The company's principal trades between Europe/Far East and Europe/Australia have been containerised within the *OCL* consortium and Ocean own and manage 5 of the containerships operated by OCL. The residual *Blue Funnel Line* dry cargo trades to the Far East are operated within *Benocean*. The round-the-world services, employing modern, multi-purpose ships, are operated within the *Barber Blue Sea Line* consortium. Elder Dempster Lines (including *Guinea Gulf Line*) operates dry cargo vessels to West Africa from UK, North Continent and USA. Blue Funnel *Bulkships* operates crude oil tankers, product tankers, combination ships and bulk carriers. The Group's Marine Division also manages ships on behalf of non-Group clients.

Ben Line

The Ben Line Steamers Limited, 33 St Mary's Street, Edinburgh EH1 1TN, is a privately owned British shipping company, operating 21 ships totalling 1,101,825 deadweight tons. The Ben Line Containers Limited is part of the organisation. The company plays a prominent part in the cargo trade between Europe and the Far East. In addition, it is active in ship management, the ownership and chartering of bulk carriers and cargo liners on world-wide routes, the operation of chemical tankers and offshore exploration drilling.

Furness Withy*

Furness Withy Group, 105 Fenchurch Street, London EC3M 5HH,owns and/or manages a fleet of 61 ships of all types totalling 1,099,115 tons deadweight, including the 9 vessels (totalling 104,700 tons deadweight) which belong to Manchester Liners Limited. Furness Withy own 62 per cent of the latter company's shares. Although Furness Withy came into being only in 1891, the brothers Christopher and Thomas Furness bought their first ship in

* Now a subsidiary of Orient Overseas Container (Holdings) Ltd., part of the C Y Tung Group of world-wide shipping interests.

1878. As the company expanded it gradually brought within its fold many well-known shipping companies, some older than Furness Withy itself. Royal Mail Lines, for example, was established in 1839. Like some other groups, Furness Withy has widened its activities beyond shipping, particularly in recent years, and the Group now controls over 100 subsidiary companies. Furness Withy is also a partner in Overseas Containers (OCL). Management, recruitment of sea staff and their employment, of the Group fleet, is now in the hands of Furness Withy (Shipping) Limited, based at 52 Leadenhall Street, London EC3A 2BR. (Manchester Liners continue to manage and crew their own vessels). The long-established trading names are maintained on the various liner routes that the Group operates: *Shaw Savill & Company Limited* is now primarily involved in a joint service with Bank Line which connects Australia and New Zealand with the Caribbean and US Gulf under the trading name of The Bank & Savill Line. *The Cairn Line of Steamships* operates a fleet of mini bulk carriers on the tramp market in the Short and Middle Seas. *Prince Line* operates conventional and container ships to the Mediterranean.

Royal Mail Lines continue to serve the East Coast of South America, a trade in which they have been involved for well over 100 years. *Pacific Steam Navigation* Company has five 'O' class vessels running regular services from the United Kingdom to the West Indies and the West coast of South America. *Houlder Brothers* have assumed responsibility for running the Group's bulk carriers and gas tankers which are employed on world-wide charters. Included in the fleet are products tankers, dry bulk carriers of up to 120,000 tons deadweight, crude oil tankers and gas tankers. *Houlder Offshore* has under its control the Group's wide-ranging and expanding offshore activities. Included are semi-submersible drilling rigs, diving operations, support vessels, and land drilling operations. *Manchester Liners Limited*, PO Box 189, Manchester Liners house, Port of Manchester, Manchester M5 2XA, operates container vessels trading between Manchester and Montreal, with a feeder service from the Great Lakes, and also into the Mediterranean.

Gatx-Oswego (UK)

Gatx-Oswego (UK) Limited, 130-135 Minories, London EC3N 1NT, manage 7 crude oil carriers totalling 1,094,954 deadweight tons.

LOF

London & Overseas Freighters Limited, 8 Balfour Place, London W1Y 6AJ, owns 6 tankers and 3 bulk carriers totalling 805,733 deadweight tons which operate worldwide.

Souter Hamlet

Souter Hamlet Limited, Clayton House, Regent Centre, Gosforth, Newcastle upon Tyne NE3 3HW, manages 13 tankers, gas tankers, chemical tankers and bulk carriers totalling 800,000 deadweight tons and operating world-wide.

Cunard

The *Cunard Steamship Company* was founded in 1840 when Samuel Cunard inaugurated trans-Atlantic mail service with the wooden paddle-wheel vessel *Britannia*, and in the early part of this century the Company expanded its shipping interests by acquiring the following companies: *The Port Line*, *T & J Brocklebank*, *H E Moss* and the *White Star Line*. *T & J Brocklebank* is one of the oldest merchant shipping companies in the world, starting trading with its own vessels over two hundred years ago in 1777. *The Port Line* was formed in 1914 by the amalgamation of four separate companies trading to Australasia. Cunard now has a fleet of 54 vessels totalling about 700,000 deadweight tons, including the offshore oil-rig supply vessels of its subsidiary, *Offshore Marine Limited*. Cunard also have a 20 per cent interest in the *Atlantic Container Line*, having four roll on/roll off container ships on the trans-Atlantic service, and a 42½ per cent interest in *Associated Container Transportation (Australia) Limited*, having three container ships in the trade to Australasia. The Company also has a service to the Middle East. Since 1971 Cunard has been a subsidiary of *Trafalgar House Limited*. The Company addresses are as follows: Cunard Line Limited, South Western House, Canute Road, Southampton; Cunard Shipping Services Limited, Trafalgar House, 2 Chalk Hill Road, Hammersmith International Centre, Hammersmith, London W6; Offshore Marine Limited, Block 3, Fish Wharf, Great Yarmouth, Norfolk. Cunard sea-going personnel are interchangeable throughout the various vessels in the fleet, and training during cadetship is carried out on all the various types of vessel.

Bibby Line

Bibby Line Limited, Norwich House, Water Street, Liverpool L2 8UW, is the oldest independent British shipping company, owning 15 dry-cargo, OBO, LPG and container ships totalling 706,572 deadweight tons.

Scottish Ship Management

Scottish Ship Management Limited, 40 Buchanan Street, Glasgow G1 3JZ, manages 16 bulk carriers totalling 404,000 deadweight tons and charters in a further 9 bulk carriers totalling 210,000 deadweight tons, all engaged in world-wide trading. The company is owned by H Hogarth & Sons Limited and Lyle Shipping Company Limited, each with a 50 per cent share.

OCL

Overseas Containers Limited, Beagle house, Braham Street, London E1 8EP, is formed by a consortium of four famous shipping lines (P&O, Furness Withy, Ocean and British & Commonwealth), and operates 17 containerships totalling some 600,000 deadweight tons.The Australian and New Zealand trade ships are managed by Container Fleets Limited, Beaufort House, Botolph Street, London EC3, and the Far East Trade ships by Ocean Fleets Limited, India Buildings, Water Street, Liverpool 2.

Vestey

This Group derives its name from the Vestey family which built it up and is still intimately concerned with it. The Group started in the shipping business with Blue Star Line, formed in 1909 to carry meat from the Argentine. A total of 38 modern vessels (totalling nearly 600,000 tons deadweight) are operated by the companies listed below. Blue Star Line is also a partner in Associated Container Transportation (Australia) Limited. One or two vessels carry a small number of passengers. *Blue Star Line Limited.* The company's head office is at Albion House, 34-35 Leadenhall Street, London EC3A 1AR, and it operates 32 refrigerated cargo and container ships on liner routes between the UK and South America; Australia, New Zealand and the Pacific Coast of North America; and Australasia and the Middle East; the company is also engaged in world-wide reefer trading. *Booth Steamship Company Limited.* The Booth Line operates from Albion House, 30 James Street, Liverpool L2 7PS, and its fleet currently consists of 2 dry cargo vessels. *Lamport & Holt Line Limited.* This company also operates from Albion house, Liverpool, currently with four ships in the South American trade. *Blue Star Ship Management Limited.* This company acts as husbandry managers for those mentioned above, also from Albion House, 30 James Street, Liverpool L2 7PS, which is the address for recruitment of sea-going personnel.

British & Commonwealth

The British & Commonwealth Shipping Company Limited, Cayzer House, 2-4 St Mary Axe, London EC3A 8EP, was formed by the merging of the interests the Union-Castle and Clan Lines. The origins of the Union-Castle Line go back to 1853. The Clan Line was formed by the Cayzer family in 1878 and this family now controls the Group. The Group fleet comprises 18 ships totalling about 581,600 deadweight tons (327,650 gross tons) and includes general cargo liners, refrigerated cargo liners, bulk carriers and products tankers. Company names include Clan Line Steamers, Houston Line, Scottish Shire Line, King Line, Scottish Tanker Company and The Union-Castle Mail

Steamship Company. The main liner trading routes are to East Africa,India and Bangladesh. Cayzer Irvine Shipping Limited, 1 Seething Lane, London EC3N 4EE, manages all the vessels within the B & C Group as well as some other companies' vessels, including the container ship *Table Bay* for OCL,in which B & C are one of the principal shareholders. The B & C Group has a number of interests other than shipping, including aviation, hotels and office equipment.

Buries Markes

Buries Markes (Ship Management) Limited, City Gate House, Finsbury Square, London EC2A 1PY, was incorporated in 1930 and is part of the world-wide Louis Dreyfus Organisation. In addition it is a member of the Gearbulk Consortium, which includes the Norwegian shipping groups Mowinckel and KG Jebsen. A further consortium was formed in 1969, under the management of Buries Markes, to own and operate chemical carriers. The company operates a fleet of 18–20 solvent and LNG tankers and bulk carriers totalling some 520,000 tons deadweight and operating world-wide. The original Argentine connections are indicated by the ear of corn on the house flag and the ships' names.

Ropner

The Ropner Shipping Company Limited, P O Box 18, Coniscliffe Road, Darlington, Co Durham DL3 7RP, own 6 ships totalling 514,546 deadweight tons. These ships are managed by Ropner Management Limited who also manage 2 ships for other owners.

Panocean-Anco

Panocean-Anco Limited, Navigation House, One Aldgate,London EC3N 1PR, operates 18 deep sea parcel tankers totalling 455,115 deadweight tons owned by Ocean Transport and Trading Limited, The Peninsular and Oriental Steam Navigation Company, Tate and Lyle Limited, John Swire & Sons Limited, Societé Française de Transports Maritimes and Malaysian International Shipping Corporation (MISC). Panocean-Anco also manages 10 tankers on behalf of associated companies.

Andrew Weir

This Group of 33 ships totalling 451,578 deadweight tons was built up by Lord Inverforth's family, the family name being Weir. *The Bank Line Limited*

(*Andrew Weir & Company Limited*–Managers), Baltic Exchange Buildings, 21 Bury Street, London EC3M 5AU, operates 25 dry cargo ships trading world-wide. *United Baltic Corporation Limited*, 24–26 Baltic Street, London EC1Y 0TB, operates 8 cargo ships to Baltic ports and Spain.

RFA

The Royal Fleet Auxiliary Service, DGST(N) Empress State Building, London SW6 1TR, operates a world-wide service supporting the Royal Navy, with food, fuel, ammunition, stores and equipment. The 30 highly sophisticated ships, totalling about 450,000 deadweight tons, include fleet replenishment ships, stores support ships, fuel tankers, ro-ros and a helicopter support ship.

Harrison Line

The Harrison Line is owned by the Charente Steam Ship Company Limited and managed by Thos & Jas Harrison Limited, Mersey Chambers, Liverpool L2 8UF. The company, which was started in 1853, is privately owned. Its 18 ships total some 400,000 deadweight tons and include dry-cargo and container ships and bulk carriers. The routes are from UK/Continent to the West Indies, Central and South America, the Gulf ports, South and East Africa and Red Sea ports.

Reardon Smith

Sir Wm Reardon Smith & Sons Limited, PO Box 90, Devonshire House, Greyfriars Road, Cardiff CF1 1RT, act as managers and brokers for the Reardon Smith Line Limited which owns 9 vessels totalling 281,000 deadweight tons. The company also act as managers for the owners of 7 further vessels totalling 114,900 deadweight tons. The Cardiff-based Reardon Smith Line dates back over 70 years and today operates a modern fleet tramping world-wide with bulk and general cargoes. Under the name of Celtic Bulk Carriers the Group is also involved in a regular service mainly in forest products from British Columbia and United States West Coast ports to UK/Continent, and in steel products from UK/Continent to the US West Coast and British Columbia.

Harrisons (Clyde)

Harrisons (Clyde) Limited, 16 Woodside Crescent, Glasgow G3 7UT, is mainly a management company though it has a substantial interest in some of the 22 vessels under its control which total about 300,000 tons deadweight. The fleet includes foreign-going bulk carriers, ro-ros, oil-rig supply vessels and ferries on the Clyde estuary.

ACT(A)

Associated Container Transportation (Australia) Limited, 136 Fenchurch Street, London EC3M 6DD, is a consortium of Blue Star Line, Cunard, T & J Harrison and Ellerman Lines associated with Australian National Line and PAD Line. The company operates 10 container vessels (7 ACT ships and 3 ANL ships) plus one ro-ro vessel, *Dilkara*. ACTs 1–7 total 208,337 deadweight tons and *Dilkara* is 20,650 deadweight tons. The routes are Europe to Australia/New Zealand, East Coast North America to Australia/New Zealand, and (PAD) West Coast North America to Australia and Pacific Islands.

Sealink

Sealink UK Limited, Eversholt House, 163–203 Eversholt Street,London NW1 1BG, is a wholly-owned subsidiary company of the British Railways Board. The company has 43 vessels, totalling some 150,032 gross tons (perhaps 225,000 deadweight tons), operating intensive services on the short sea routes to the Continent, Ireland, the Channel Islands and the Isle of Wight. The majority of the ships are multi-purpose, carrying lorries, cars and passengers, and there are some specialist ro-ro, train ferry and container ships.

Common Brothers

The Common Brothers Group, Bamburgh House, Market Street, Newcastle upon Tyne NE1 6JU, was established in 1893 and owns or manages a fleet of 12 vessels totalling 222,027 tons deadweight. Management is vested in Common Brothers (Management) Limited and is on behalf of The Northumbrian Shipping Company Limited, Rachid Fares Enterprises Limited, Cementos Anahuac Del Golfo, Atlas Societé Marocaine de Navigation and others. The ship types include product carriers, livestock carriers, dry cargo ships and bulk cement carriers. They trade world-wide but mostly in the Atlantic Basin, Mediterranean and Indian Ocean areas.

Salvesen

Christian Salvesen (Shipping) Limited, 50 East Fettes Avenue,Edinburgh EH4 1EQ, is part of the Christian Salvesen Group which has building and other transport interests. The company owns and manages 14 ships totalling

127,000 tons gross (perhaps 190,000 tons deadweight) engaged in coastal and deepsea trades and in oil rig supply.

Salén UK

Salén UK Ship Management Limited, 19 Grange Road, London SE1 3BT, is part of the Salén Group, Stockholm, and was formerly known as Whitco Marine Services Limited. The company owns or manages 8 ships–bulk carriers and refrigerated vessels–totalling 170,000 tons deadweight. The ships operate world-wide, some being engaged in season in the Moroccan fruit trade.

Stephenson Clarke

Stephenson Clarke Shipping Limited, Europe House, World Trade Centre, London E1 9AJ, is a member of the Powell Duffryn Group, owning 36 ships and managing 10 more (mostly on behalf of the Central Electricity Generating Board), the total deadweight tonnage being 165,370. The ships are bulk carriers, tankers and waste disposal hopper barges operating on the UK coast, in north-west Europe and in the Mediterranean.

Ellerman

Ellerman Lines Limited was built up by the first Sir John Ellerman with the acquisition of Hall Line, The City Line, Papayanni Line and Westcott & Lawrence Line in 1901, the Bucknall Line in 1908 and the Wilson Line in 1916. A major reorganisation in 1973 resulted in the formation of a shipping division to take over and manage the trades and ships of the Ellerman Lines. The Group's other interests include breweries, international travel and leisure and road transport. The Group owns 7 ships and is a partner in Associated Container Transportation (Australia) Limited, Ben Line Containers Limited, and Ellerman Harrison Container Line. *Ellerman City Liners* (the shipping division of Ellerman Lines), 12–20 Camomile Street, London EC3A 7EX, operates 8 cargo and container ships. The routes are from UK/Continent to serve Portugal and Mediterranean ports, and maintain regular services to South and East Africa, the Red Sea ports, Aden, the Arabian Gulf and the principal ports in India, Pakistan and Ceylon. Other services bridge the eastern and western hemispheres, linking Australia and New Zealand with North America through ACT(A); also Sri Lanka, India, Pakistan, Bangladesh. *EWL* is the transport division of Ellerman Lines, and operates roll-on/roll-off vessels on the North Sea. Total tonnage is about 150,000 deadweight tons.

Hudson

Hudson Steamship Company Limited, 8 Maltravers Street, London WC2R 3EQ, manage 2 ships totalling 127,000 tons deadweight.

Haverton Shipping

Haverton Shipping Limited, Portsoken House, 155–157 Minories, London EC3N 1BB, own 4 ships totalling about 120,000 tons deadweight carrying containers and break-bulk, trading between Africa and the Far East.

Palm Line

Palm Line, UAC House, PO Box 2, Blackfriars Road, London SE1 9UG, is a subsidiary of Unilever and owns 9 ships totalling 67,189 tons gross (about 100,000 tons deadweight). The company operates a liner service in the West African trade.

Hunting

Hunting & Son Limited, PO Box 1TA Milburn house, Newcastle upon Tyne NE99 1TA, are owners or managers of 4 ships totalling some 100,000 tons deadweight, all of them self-discharging bulk carriers.

Blandford

Blandford Shipping Company Limited, Blackfriars House, 19 New Bridge Street, London EC4V 6DB, is owned by the Norwegian Fred Olsen & Company, and owns 4 ships, some bulk carriers totalling 100,000 tons deadweight.

Turnbull Scott

Turnbull Scott Management Limited, Abbey House, Farnborough Road, Farnborough, Hants GU14 7ND, own or manage 15 ships totalling 96,967 deadweight tons which tramp world-wide.

James Fisher

James Fisher & Sons Limited, P O Box 4, Fisher House, Barrow-in-Furness LA14 HR, own 27 ships totalling 60,512 tons gross (about 90,000 tons deadweight), most of them coastal or in the shortsea trades. The company are specialists in the carriage of heavy machinery and abnormal loads.

Everard

F T Everard & Sons Limited, The Wharf, Greenhithe, Kent DA9 9NW, owns 43 ships, both dry cargo ships and tankers, totalling 88,534 deadweight tons. Most of the ships operate on the coast or in the shortsea trades, but the larger ships trade world-wide.

Bowring

The Bowring Steamship Company Limited, St Johns House, 124–127 Minories, London EC3N 1TQ, is part of the Bowring Group and is a company that has owned ships for over 150 years. The company now operates 3 modern geared bulk carriers totalling 81,530 tons deadweight.

Graig Shipping

The Graig Shipping Company Limited, 113–116 Bute Street, Cardiff CF1 6TE, owns 2 ships totalling 80,979 tons deadweight.

Stag Line

Stag Line Limited, 1 Howard Street, North Shields, Tyne and Wear NE30 1NE, owns 4 ships totalling 80,228 tons deadweight and operating world-wide.

Jebsens (UK)

Jebsens (UK) Limited, 53–55 High Street, Ruislip, Middlesex HA4 7BK, are part of the Norwegian company Kristian A/S Jebsens Rederi and manage 8 ships totalling about 73,000 tons deadweight.

Fyffes

Fyffes Group Limited, 1 Queens Way, Southampton SO1 1AQ, dates back to 1901 and is a sister company of United Brands Company, New York. The 12 refrigerated cargo vessels, totalling 67,000 tons deadweight, operate world-wide, *Bayano* and *Barranca*, delivered in 1973, being the first fully refrigerated banana container ships in the world.

Bolton Steam

The Bolton Steam Shipping Company Limited, The Corn Exchange Building, 52–57 Mark Lane, London EC3R 7ST, owns 2 ships totalling 60,000 tons deadweight.

Rowbotham

C Rowbotham & Sons (Management) Limited, Abbey House, Farnborough, Hampshire, a subsidiary of Ingram Corporation, New Orleans, owns 19 ships totalling 59,820 tons deadweight. The ships are mostly small, carrying petroleum or chemicals in bulk.

Comben Longstaff

Comben Longstaff & Company Limited, 24 St Mary Axe, London EC3A 8EQ, owns 9 ships totalling some 34,000 tons deadweight. They are general traders to the Continent, Baltic and Mediterranean.

Geest Line

The Geest Line, No 2 Dock, Barry, Glamorgan CF6 6XP, part of Geest Industries Limited which is a subsidiary of Geest Holdings Limited, owns 4 ships totalling 30,036 tons deadweight. Geest Line operates fruit-carriers on a weekly service to Barbados and the Windward Islands.

West Hartlepool

The West Hartlepool Steam Navigation Company Limited, 4 Church Square, Hartlepool, Cleveland TS24 7EL, owns 2 ships totalling 30,000 tons deadweight which engage in world-wide trading, either on voyage or time charter. The company has existed for more than 123 years.

Booker Line

Booker Line Limited, Martins Building, Liverpool L2 3TE, owns 4 ships totalling 27,900 tons deadweight. The company is part of the Shipping Division of Booker McConnell Limited.

Cable & Wireless

Cable & Wireless Limited, Mercury House, Theobalds Road, London WC1X 8RX, owns 5 ships totalling 24,047 tons deadweight, the largest single fleet of cable ships in the world. In its present form the company dates from 1934 but its origins go back to the mid-19th century. The ships operate world-wide.

Runciman

Walter Runciman & Company Limited, 52 Leadenhall Street, London EC3A 2BH, owns Anchor Line Limited, 59 Waterloo Street, Glasgow G2 7BU, which in turn controls 2 cargo liners totalling 23,450 deadweight tons and ten small liquefied gas carriers. Recruitment is through its subsidiaries, Anchor Line Ship Management and George Gibson & Company.

The Merchant Navy in perspective

In the 400 years that have elapsed since Sir Francis Drake made his famous circumnavigation of the world the British merchant fleet has increased in size from approximately 50,000 tons to some 27,000,000 tons. Since the earlier figure is estimated in tons burden and the latter in tons gross, the modern figure would need to be increased to make the two strictly comparable. The increase has been some 600-fold and, given the increased speed and diminished turn-round time of the ships of today, it is probably true to say that one fair-sized modern bulk carrier could carry as much as the entire merchant fleet of Queen Elizabeth I.

In these same 400 years the average size of ships has increased about 80-fold and the typical size of a large ship has gone up from 200 tons to about 30,000 tons.

Despite this enormous increase in the size of ships, the typical ship's crew is hardly more numerous than it was when the Armada sailed the seas. During the first years of the 17th century a 160-ton ship would carry a crew of 25, a 200-ton ship a crew of 30, and a 450-ton East Indiaman a crew of 89. In other words there was at least one member of the crew for every seven tons of carrying capacity. By the middle of the 18th century a 120-ton ship was carrying a crew of only 9 and a 200-ton ship a crew of only 13. The ratio of crew to size had halved, with about one crew member for every 15 tons of carrying capacity. By the middle of the 19th century the ratio of the crew to size had halved again and one crew member was carried for every 35 tons or so.

Taking the Merchant Navy as a whole, the proportion nowadays is one crew member for 330 tons, a figure which is three times what it was a generation ago and ten times what it was in early Victorian times.

In the days of Samuel Pepys, when Britain had rather more than 200,000 tons of merchant shipping, there appear to have been about 30,000 seafarers though probably not all of them were in employment. At the beginning of the present century there were eight times as many. Now there are fewer than three times as many although the merchant fleet is 135 times larger than it was when Pepys was alive.

The modern ship makes about six round trips to the Far East in the time taken by a ship in Pepys's time. In other words, even if it were the same size as the early East Indiaman, the modern ship could lift six times as much cargo in the same period. On the shorter sea-routes the proportionate rate of turn-round of the modern ship is greater still. In terms of goods carried, the 'productivity' of the modern seafarer seems to be 300 times greater than it was in Elizabethan times, even though the seafarer works less hard and his conditions of work are far safer and far more agreeable than they were at the time of the privateering voyages. To put this another way, the modern seafarer will achieve in his lifetime more than would be achieved by the crews of eighteen complete ships in the days of Elizabeth I. The explanation, of course, is to be found in the tremendous advance since Elizabethan times in the general standard of education, in naval architecture, and in engineering and business techniques.

The past seventy years

In 1914 the world merchant fleet totalled just under 50 million gross tons and of this total Britain possessed nearly 20 million tons.

Now, world merchant shipping amounts to 431 million gross tons (680 million deadweight tons), to which the British contribution is 27 million tons. In a seventy-year period in which the world fleet has increased more than eight-fold, the British fleet has grown by only 35 per cent.

Some of the reasons for the slow growth in the British merchant fleet in the thirty years that followed the First World War are to be found in Britain's pre-eminent position before that war. Britain was the first country to develop the ocean-going steamship and it was only after 1890 that other industrial countries began to make rapid progress. Between the two world wars Britain's export trade in coal declined and, although the trade in oil was expanding, Britain did not become immediately so dependent upon oil imports as did some other countries. In consequence of these changes in the nature of trade some foreign maritime countries began to make rather faster progress than Britain.

Since the Second World War many new nations have striven to build up merchant fleets, in some cases for political rather than for economic reasons. By the end of the 1960's Britain was no longer able to lay claim–as she had done for a century and a half–to being the world's premier maritime nation. Fleets registered under the Liberian, Japanese and Greek flags now greatly exceed the British fleet in size, the Liberian fleet (much of it American-owned) being three times the British tonnage.

Many ships nowadays are registered in countries other than that of the owners of the vessel and fly the flag of the country of registration. Such ships are said to fly 'flags of convenience'. This use of such flags is largely a post-World War II phenomenon, and there are two reasons for their use: firstly the profits made by ships flying flags of convenience are lightly taxed or not taxed at all; and secondly the shipowner is thus able to operate and man ships without being subject to the laws of his own country. Generally speaking, the flag of convenience ship can employ the cheapest seafarers. It is also subject to

ACT (A)

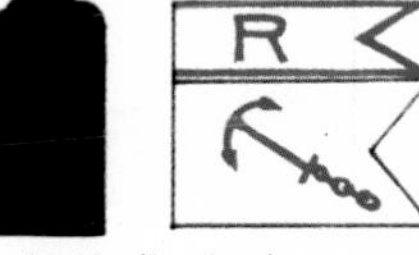

Anchor Line (Runciman)

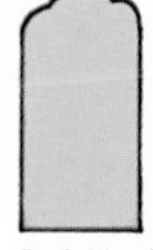

Bank Line (Andrew Weir)

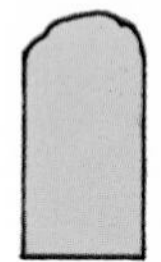

Ben Line

Bibby Line

Blue Funnel (Ocean)

Blue Star Line (Vestey))

Bolton SS

Bowring

B & C (Clan Funnel)

BP

Buries Markes

CP

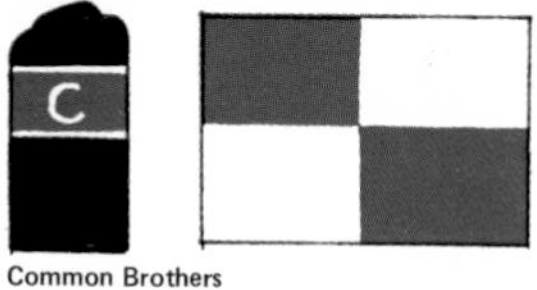

Common Brothers

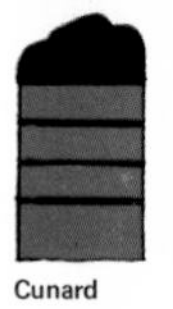

Cunard

Denholm

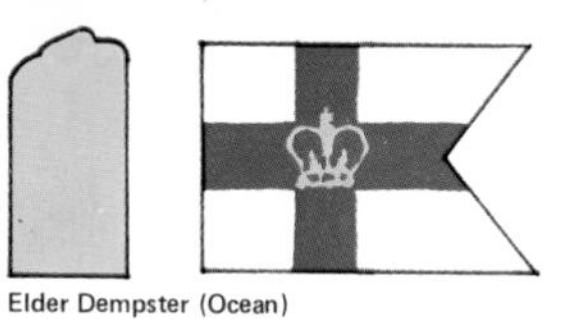

Elder Dempster (Ocean)

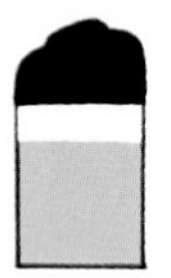
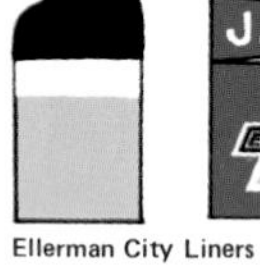

Ellerman City Liners

Esso

Everard

Fyffes Line

Geest Line

Harrison Line

Harrisons (Clyde)

Houlder Bros (Furness Withy)

Hudson SS

Hunting

London & Overseas Freighters

Mobil

Manchester Liners (Furness Withy)

OCL

Palm Line

Panocean–Anco

PSNC (Furness Withy)

P & O

Reardon Smith

Ropner

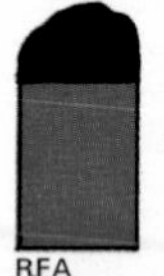

RFA

Salen UK

Chr. Salvesen

Scottish Ship Management

Sealink

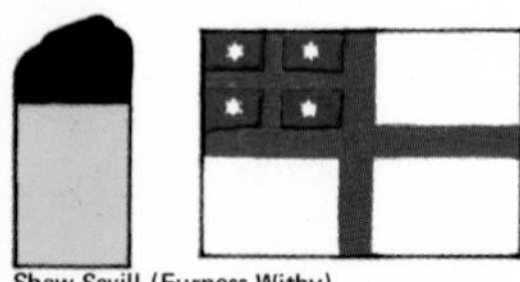
Shaw Savill (Furness Withy)

Shell

Silver Line

Stag Line

Texaco

Turnbull Scott

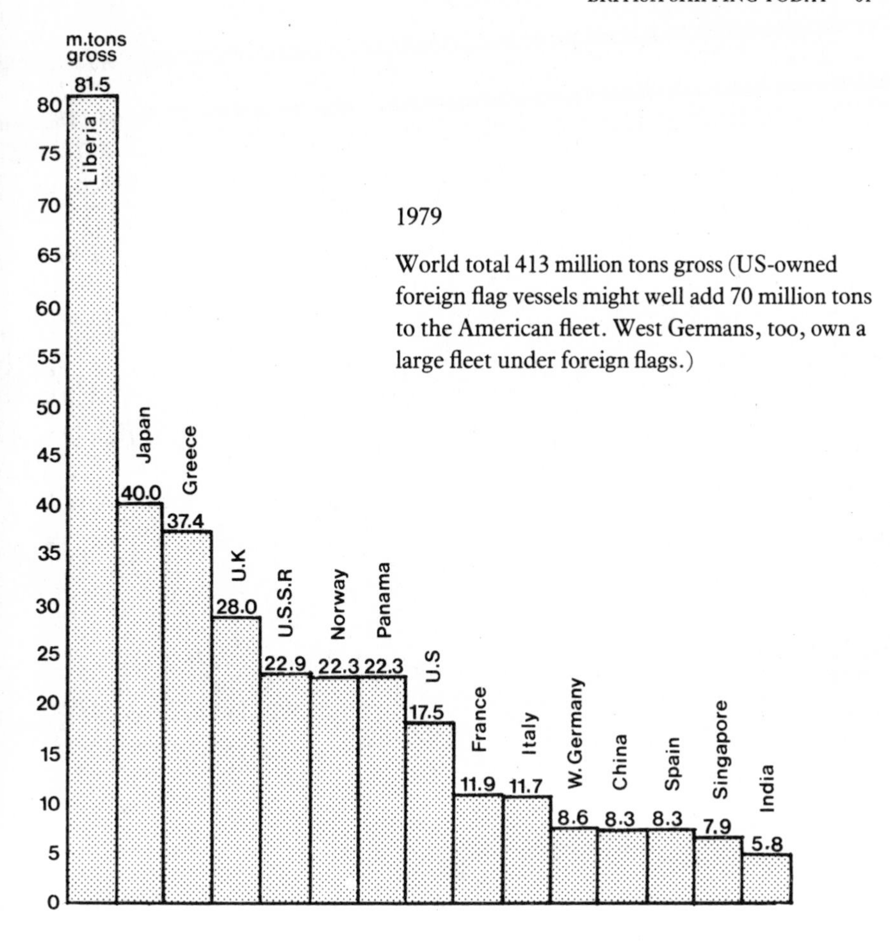

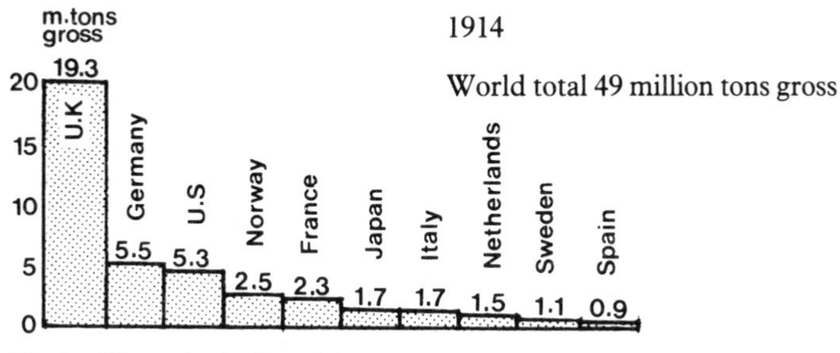

Fig 8 The principal maritime powers

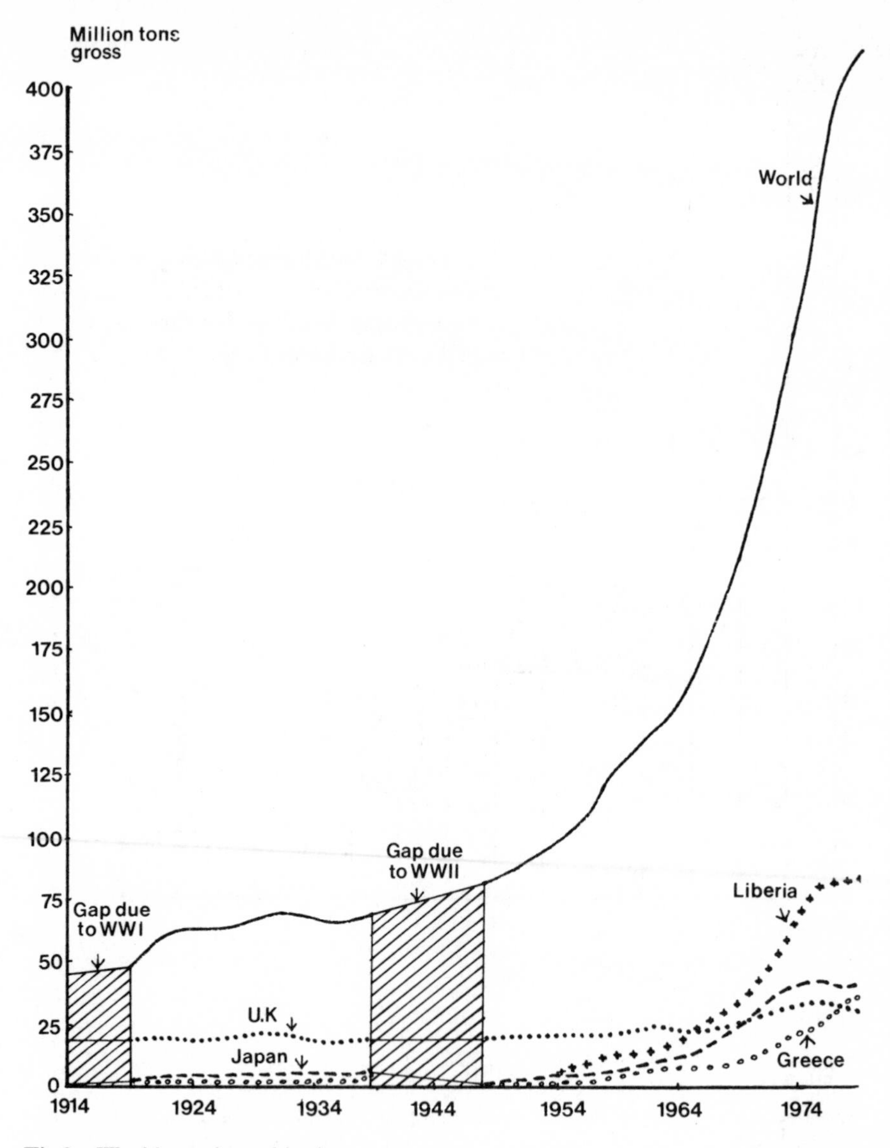

Fig 9 World merchant shipping

less government regulation. Even where the standards of operation are generally high financial advantages will accrue to those who can 'bend the rules' when it suits them to do so. That the use of flags of convenience pays some operators is clear from the statistics. In negligible use forty years ago, convenience flags now fly over more than 30 per cent of the world's shipping.

To establish a genuine link between convenience countries and convenience ships, as the 1958 United Nations Law of the Sea Conference demanded, is difficult. In the *Torrey Canyon* case–where large areas of coast and sea were polluted by shipwreck due to bad navigation–a ship owned by the Barracuda Tanker Corporation of Bermuda and registered in Liberia was under lease to the Union Oil Company of California, which had sub-leased the ship to British Petroleum Trading Limited, a subsidiary of BP. The crew was Italian and the true owners were never identified. After repeated failures to obtain compensation for the damage done, or even consideration, through the courts, the British and French Governments eventually collected £7,500,000 from her London insurers when British Treasury agents seized the sister ship, *Lake Palourde*, in Singapore and issued an arrest writ against her.

That the use of convenience flags can mask unsafe operation may be illustrated by the loss with all her crew of the Liberia-registered cargo ship *Seagull* (6,507 tons gross) in 1974. The master was the only qualified bridge watchkeeper; the mate had been promoted from the position of radio officer; there was no second mate; and there were no qualified engineer officers.

The other factor which increases the complexity of modern merchant shipping and its operation is the degree to which some nations are prepared to subsidise national fleets and national shipbuilding industries.

The ways in which ships should be licensed, taxed and properly regulated in the interests of the world at large have yet to be worked out. On the one hand there are the multi-national concerns, with finance supplied by the rich industrial countries, which increasingly seek to operate ships under convenience flags and man them with cheap seafarers. On the other hand there are the poorer countries which seek to establish their own merchant fleets and demand that they carry at least 40 per cent of their trade irrespective of cost. The type of 19th-century shipowner who built up the British fleet in conditions of 'laissez-faire' is hard put to it to survive in these conditions, especially when heavily-subsidised communist country fleets compete in his traditional trades.

Bearing all this in mind it is difficult to avoid the conclusion that shipping will become increasingly subject to government control, and that the world is moving towards a situation where shipping will come to resemble air transport with each country laying claim to a fleet related to the size of its trade. In such circumstances the British-flag fleet would probably be much the size it is now, provided British trade remains at its present level.

3 Entry and Advancement

Where lies the land to which the ship would go?
Far, far ahead, is all her seamen know.
A H Clough

Any seafarer with ability and a willingness to work can go far, far ahead. There is no bar to advancement in any branch of the Merchant Navy.

The General Council of British Shipping, through its British Shipping Careers Service, 30–32 St Mary Axe, London EC3A 8ET, issues free literature on the Merchant Navy as a career and has branch offices in major ports. It offers advice and, on behalf of different shipping companies, handles many applications for employment at sea.

The major shipping groups issue their own free literature on entry and careers and have special departments dealing with recruitment and training. *The Directory of Shipowners, Shipbuilders & Marine Engineers*, annually by *Marine Week* and available in most reference libraries, lists all shipping companies, giving addresses, names of ships, brief details of trades and names of principal officials. Prospective navigating and engineer cadets may seek advice from the Merchant Navy and Airline Officers Association. The Institute of Marine Engineers, 76 Mark Lane, London EC3R 7JN, issues a free booklet on marine engineering as a profession, and employs an Education and Training Officer who will offer advice. Prospective radio officers can seek advice from the Radio and Electronic Officers Union. Advice and information on the Merchant Navy are also available from The Marine Society.

It is a good idea to seek advice and information from more than one source before taking a decision. It is also as well to check on the required standard of fitness and, in the deck or navigating department, on the required standard of vision. Prospective deck cadets are officially recommended to undergo a thorough examination of their sight by an ophthalmologist before embarking on a sea career.

Although it can provide an excellent career for the right man, the sea is not a life for everyone. It is expensive for both the industry and the individual entrant to train the wrong man.

Basic conditions of employment in the Merchant Navy are agreed by the National Maritime Board and published in a Summary of Agreements. Pension schemes exist, and paid leave takes cognisance of the fact that seafarers spend seven days a week at sea–four month's leave or more in the year is not uncommon. Salary figures go rapidly out of date, but it can be assumed that Merchant Navy rates of pay compare well with those ashore for posts demanding similar skills. Many companies offer conditions above the basic ones agreed by the NMB, though this may be in part compensation for conditions in a particular trade. The master of a large vessel can earn more than a university professor.

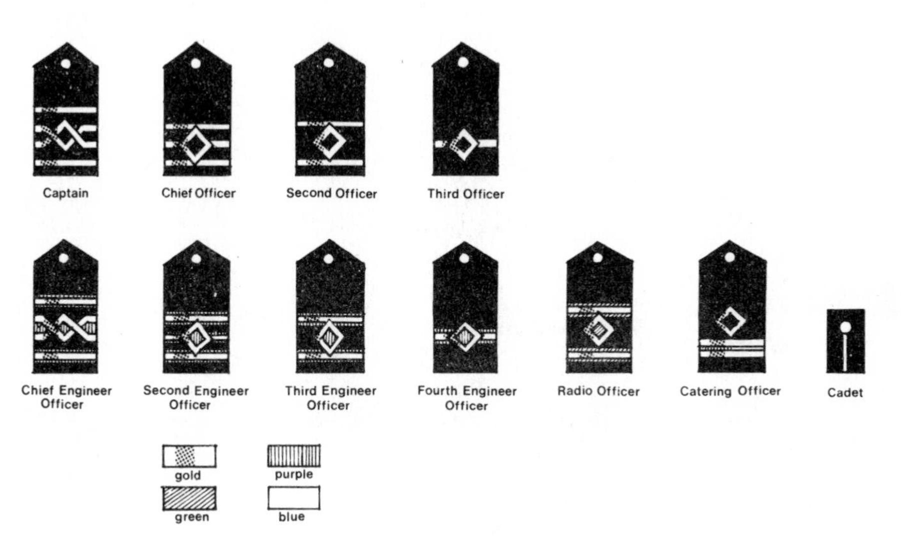

Fig 10 Merchant Navy badges of rank

Entry as a rating

Applicants for entry into the Merchant Navy as junior seamen or catering ratings must be United Kingdom citizens resident with their parents or guardians (from whom consent must be obtained), and they must be able to swim. The minimum age at which application will be considered is 15½ and the maximum age at which training can begin is 17¼ (subject to alteration). Applicants should be medically and dentally fit, with physique adequate for the demands of life at sea. Weight should be compatible with age and height. A medical examination is part of the selection process, and all trainees are vaccinated and inoculated. Perfect form and colour vision without aids is necessary for junior seamen, though glasses may be worn by junior catering ratings in the catering department provided the applicant reaches the required standard, in form vision, thus equipped and possesses two pairs of glasses.

There are no formal educational requirements, though the better educated are preferred. Those junior seamen with 3 CSE passes at grade 3 or above (to

Progression shown is on the basis of
DoT Safe Manning Regulations
Further advancement to officer status possible,
according to enthusiasm and ability to obtain
a DoT Certificate of Competency.
↑
Chief Petty Officer
↑
Petty Officer
↑
Seaman Grade I
(after validation of AB certificate)
↑
Seaman Grade II
(after validation of EDH certificate)
↑
Seaman Grade III (14½ months)
↑
Seaman Trainee (2 months)
(EDH and Lifeboatman certificate)
↑
National Sea Training College

Fig 11 Ladder of promotion in the GP scheme

include mathematics, physics and English or kindred subjects) may be offered special training to enable them to qualify as navigating officers. The maximum age of entry for this course can be extended to 18¼.

On entry, through the British Shipping Careers Service, junior seamen and catering ratings are trained at the National Sea Training College, Gravesend, Kent. The first four weeks of training comprise a safety course; thereafter the junior seamen's course lasts a further 10 weeks and the catering course a further 6 weeks, the latter being a course largely concerned with the duties of a steward but with some basic cookery. The course is free and railway warrents are provided to cover the cost of travel on joining and leaving. An initial issue of uniform is also free. A few young men enter the industry direct from the TS (training ship) *Indefatigable* on Anglesey where a two-term residential course is provided from the age of 15¼. It is also possible for those with suitable experience, eg in the Royal Navy or in the catering industry ashore, to join the Merchant Navy later in life.

Prospective engine-room ratings (motormen) must be between 19 and 30 years of age and undertake a three-week entry course at the Adult Engineroom Ratings Training Centre, Mann Island, Liverpool.

CATERING OFFICER
(Purser/Chief Steward)

Direct responsibility to Master for all catering arrangements. Plans menus. Orders and controls the use of catering stores. Responsible for the issue and administration of bond and slop chest (shop) and medical locker. Must hold MNTB/NEBSS Catering Officer Officer's certificate.

CHIEF COOK

In charge of galley operations. Must be proficient at butchery and breadmaking. Familiar with company scale of provisions. Responsible for cleanliness of galley and cold rooms. Understudies Catering Officer. Must hold DoT Ship Cook's certificate. Higher grade after two years.

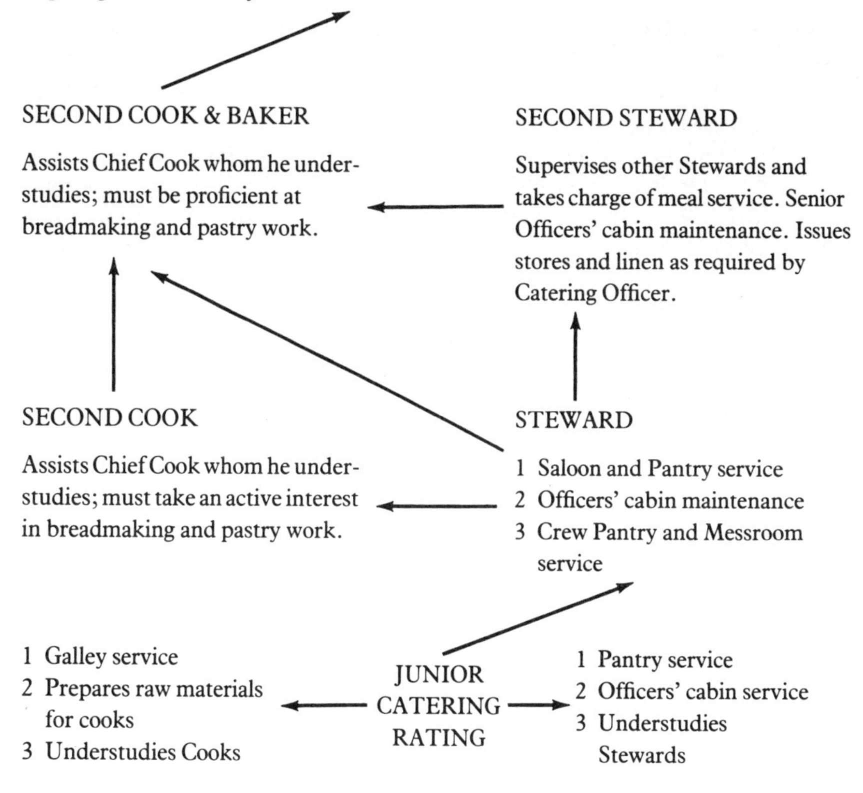

Fig 12 The catering department tree
A promotion chart applicable to many merchant ships

On completion of training, all ratings join the Merchant Navy Established Service Scheme whereby they are appointed to different ships but they may, if they so wish, apply for a contract with a particular shipping company.

During their time at Gravesend all junior seamen are examined for the Department of Trade's certificate as an Efficient Deck Hand and as Lifeboatman. The certificates are not awarded until the successful candidate is 18 years of age and has completed at least twelve months sea service, but there is no further examination as he progresses from Junior Seaman to Seaman (Grade II) to Seaman (Grade I) and perhaps to Petty Officer and Chief Petty Officer. There is no bar to a seaman becoming qualified as a watchkeeping officer if he has the required ability and sea service but to do so he has to pass the requisite Department of Trade examinations. Young men who have such ambitions are advised to join the voluntary educational classes at Gravesend and to make contact with The Marine Society since this organisation will endeavour to help them.

The catering rating may readily aspire to become a Catering Officer. Like their counterparts in the deck department, stewards under training at Gravesend are entered for the DoT certificate examination for Lifeboatman. Promotion from Junior Catering Rating to Steward or Cook Assistant normally occurs at about 18 years of age but can be earlier. Thereafter promotion on the stewarding side follows a short course leading to a Merchant Navy Training Board (MNTB) certificate for Second Stewards. On the cooking side promotion follows the passing of statutory examinations for Ship's Cook; there are two such examinations, following in each case upon a full-time six-week course. The head of the catering department of a foreign-going vessel (excluding passenger ships) with a normal complement of over 20 persons is required to hold an MNTB Catering Officer's Certificate. This is obtained after a further full-time six-week course. The Marine Society can provide relevant books for study at sea and such ancillary correspondence courses as book-keeping.

In the engine-room promotion to petty officer rank is made from among experienced ratings (motormen) without examination. It is possible for the engine-room rating to qualify as an engineer officer (or, in certain cases, mechanic) after a period of service at sea by embarking upon a special shore course, but the better his general education, particularly in mathematics and science, the easier he will find this to achieve. If he has officer status in view and if his general education is deficient when he embarks upon a sea career, he will find it advisable to study by correspondence with the help of The Marine Society (College of the Sea).

Nowadays, some shipping companies employ general purpose (GP) ratings capable of working both on deck and in the engine-room. These are recruited from among the ratings of both departments and given special training. They earn more when employed on GP ships but revert to their original rating and pay on conventionally manned ships.

Fig 13 Principal Companies accepting Cadets
(also indicating whether they employ their own radio officers or take them from other sources, and where the ratings originate)

COMPANY	ACCEPTS NAVIGATING CADETS	ACCEPTS ENGINEER CADETS	SOURCE OF RADIO OFFICERS	UK RATINGS	NON-DOMICILED RATINGS
Anchor Line	yes	yes	Marconi	all	
Bank Line	yes	yes	Marconi IMR		all
Ben Line	yes*	yes	Marconi	mostly	some
Bibby Line	yes	yes	own	some	some
Blandford Shipping	yes	yes	own	all	
Blue Star (Vestey)	yes*†	yes	IMR	mostly	some
Bolton S S	yes	yes	Marconi, IMR	all	
Booker Line	yes		IMR	all	
Bowring	yes	yes	Marconi	all	
B & C	yes	yes	own	mostly	some
BP	yes	yes	own‡	mostly	some
Buries Markes	yes	yes	own	all	
CP	yes	yes	own	mostly	some
Common Brothers	yes	yes	own	some	mostly
Cunard	yes	yes	own	some	some
Denholm	yes	yes	own; Marconi	some	some
Ellerman	yes	yes	Marconi	some	mostly
Esso	yes	yes	not own	all	
Everard	yes	yes		all	
Furness Withy	yes	yes	own; Marconi	all	
Fyffes	yes*	yes*	own	mostly	some
Graig Shipping	yes	yes	Kelvin Hughes; Redifon	all	
Harrison Line	yes	yes	Marconi	all	
Harrisons (Clyde)	yes	yes	Marconi, IMR	all	
LOF	yes	yes	own		all

Mobil	yes	yes	Marconi	some	mostly
Ocean	yes*	yes	own	some	some
OCL	yes	yes	own	all	
Palm Line	yes	yes	Marconi	some	some
Panocean-Anco	yes	yes	own	all	
P&O	yes	yes	own	some	some
Reardon Smith	yes	yes	radio cadets		all
Ropner	yes	yes	Marconi, IMR	all	
Rowbotham	yes		UME	all	
RFA	yes	yes	own	all	
Salén UK	yes	yes	IMR	few	mostly
Salvesen	yes	yes	own	some (short-sea)	some (deep-sea)
SSM	yes	yes	own	all	
Sealink			own	all	
Shell	yes	yes	own‡	mostly	some
Silver Line	yes	yes	own	some	some
Souter Hamlet	yes	yes	part own	some	some
Stag Line	yes	yes	Marconi	all	
Stephenson Clarke		yes	part own	all	
Texaco	yes	yes	Marconi	some	some
Turnbull Scott	yes	yes	not own	all	
West Hartlepool	yes		Marconi	all	

*A-level entry as well as O-level
†Graduate entry as well as O-level
‡May take radio cadets

(fig 13)

Deck or navigating officers

The customary way to the command of a ship is by starting as a navigating or deck cadet. Entry is normally between the ages of 16 and 19, though initial application can be made before the age of 16 is reached and before GCE examination results are known. The British Shipping Careers Service can arrange cadetships with many British companies but direct application may also be made to a chosen company. A medical examination must be passed, and deck cadets must have normal vision in both form and colour and be able to pass the Department of Trade's sight test.

The preferred minimum qualification for a navigating cadetship is four GCE O-levels (or equivalent) including mathematics, a science (ideally physics) and two other subjects, one of which must demonstrate ability in the use of English (English language, literature, history, etc).

Qualifications determine the level of course taken. The courses are streamed and above-minimum qualifications (eg A levels) may enable a cadet to get on faster. The normal cadetship lasts 3½ to 4 years, at the end of which time the cadet should have gained his TEC (Technician Education Council) or SCOTEC (Scottish TEC) Diploma in Nautical Science as well as a Department of Trade Class 4 certificate. If both are obtained successfully he is awarded a DoT Class 3 certificate without further examination. (There is a lower certificate than these to which seafarers can aspire, Class 5, but the use of the qualification achieved is restricted to ships under 5000grt–gross registered tons–operating in the middle and near-Continental trades.)

The pre-sea induction course for a navigating cadet (*Phase I*) is normally only two weeks in duration. This course is held at a nautical college to which the cadet returns for further periods of training after periods spent at sea. The rest of the normal 'sandwich' is as follows: *Phase II*, 10—12 months at sea, following a guided programme of shipboard study; *Phase III*, 38 weeks at college, during which time the cadet should obtain his DoT certificates as Efficient Deck Hand and Lifeboatman, his RRTO (Restricted Radio-Telephone Operator) certificate, a first-aid certificate, his Navaids (navigational aids) certificate, and his TEC Diploma, which exempts him from the mathematics, science and principles of navigation papers in the Class 3 certificate examination; *Phase IV*, 12 months at sea, following a guided programme of shipboard study and completing certain tasks set by the Merchant Navy Training Board; *Phase V*, 14 weeks at college, during which time he should obtain his Class 4 and Radar observer's certificates. *Phase VI*, 4–6 months at sea, after which the Class 3 certificate is awarded. Study time is allowed in normal working hours at sea, and throughout this period the cadet is on pay.

A limited number of entrants follow a 5-year sandwich course leading to a BSc degree in Nautical Science as well as to the DoT Class 3 certificate. Entry requirements at age 18 or 19 are at least five GCE passes of which two must be at A-level. Mature seafarers may qualify for entry to a degree course by way of the TEC Diploma or by way of their DoT certificates plus proven competency in mathematics (eg an A-level pass which may be obtained at sea with help from The Marine Society). The degree is broadly-based and has uses ashore as well as at sea.

Applications for admission to degree courses should be addressed to the appropriate university or polytechnic, namely: University of Wales Institute of Science and Technology; Southampton (or College of Nautical Studies, Warsash); Plymouth Polytechnic; Liverpool Polytechnic; and Sunderland Polytechnic. Some of the courses require industrial experience at sea and applicants should, therefore, ensure they are able to meet the industry's standards. It is also advisable to secure an offer of employment for the industrial phases from a company prior to entry.

One or two shipping companies also recruit as trainee deck officers graduates with degrees in other disciplines. Special enquiry should be made of the British Shipping Careers Service or The Marine Society.

At one time it was normal for those wishing to pursue a career at sea, particularly as a deck officer, to embark upon nautical training at an early age. This is no longer necessary, but in Hull and London there are day secondary schools with a nautical bias for boys who are attracted to such schooling.

Engineer officers

The shipping industry will accept as junior engineer officers young men who have satisfactorily completed four years engineering training ashore. This period of service may include full time education between the ages of 16 and 17; it must include one year 'off-the-job' training in the use of tools and techniques of general engineering practice at an industrial training centre either approved by the Engineering Industry Training Board or to its standards. Application should be made before completion of training either to the British Shipping Careers Service or to a shipping company.

For direct entry to shipping as an engineer officer cadet an applicant should be between 16 and 18½ years of age. Under this scheme the education and training is sponsored and financed by a shipping company, and application may be made to either the British Shipping Careers Service or to a chosen company. A medical examination must be passed, and engineer cadets must have normal vision, with glasses if necessary, and pass a modified colour vision test.

The cadetship (on pay) is of four years' duration and includes: *Phase I*, two years college-based education and workshop training; *Phase II*, one year shipboard service following a progressive programme of training; and *Phase III*, one year of college based training designed to consolidate the practical training experience gained during Phases I and II. The Technician Education Council (TEC) or the Scottish Technician Education Council (SCOTEC) Diploma examinations are taken during Phase I and the TEC or SCOTEC Higher Diploma or Certificate is taken in Phase III.

The particular course followed will depend upon the qualifications held by the cadet. The minimum requirement for entry to the TEC or SCOTEC Diploma course is four awards in CSE including mathematics Grade1, physics or an acceptable science subject Grade 1 and English language Grade 3. There is normally competition for cadetships and the majority of those accepted hold four or more GCE O-level passes (Grades A–C), including the three subjects mentioned above.

A variation on the above scheme provides for a limited number of entrants holding GCE A-level passes in mathematics and/or physics (preferably both) to embark on courses which result in the award of the Higher National Diploma in Mechanical Engineering (Marine) or a degree in Marine Engineering.

All cadets completing the full four year cadetship will be eligible for immediate entry to the examination for the Department of Trade's Certificate of Competency (Marine Engineer Officer) Class 4. In addition cadets successfully passing the TEC/SCOTEC Higher Certificate will be granted exemptions from part of the Department of Trade's Class 2 certificate examination and those passing the Higher Diploma may have these exemptions extended to the Class 1 examinations.

Additional information

Cadet pay is related to age and service, and course fees and college residential costs are covered by the employer. The major item of personal expense is the cost of clothing, but interest-free loans for this purpose are available from The Marine Society and grants are made to cadets in case of hardship.

At the conclusion of training a cadet can expect to be appointed a junior officer. Thereafter, to attain the highest ranks, he will need to obtain the higher certificates awarded by the Department of Trade–Certificates 2 and 1. Periods of paid study leave are given for this purpose, and necessary textbooks are avaliable from The Marine Society. The DoT also conducts voluntary examinations for an Extra Master's Certificate for navigating officers and for an Extra First Class Certificate for engineer officers. For certain purposes these certificates are equivalent to a first degree. There may be opportunities, after appropriate studies, for the engineer officer to become a Chartered Engineer, a qualification which carries degree status.

The speed of promotion varies from company to company and from time to time, but it is not uncommon to find chief engineer officers of large ocean-going ships in their early thirties and masters in their early forties. For both there are the opportunities to come ashore in a managerial capacity.

Radio and electronic officers

Those who wish to become radio officers must be over 16 (and under about 30) when they begin training and should preferably have GCE O-level passes in mathematics, physics, one other science and English. There is a medical examination; the wearing of glasses is permitted, but candidates must pass a modified colour vision test and hearing must be free of defects. Radio officers in British ships are required to be British subjects.

Many shipping companies have contracts for the supply of both radio officers and equipment with one or other of the following companies: Marconi International Marine Co Ltd, Elettra House, Westway, Chelmsford CM1

3BH; International Marine Radio Co Ltd, Commonside East, Mitcham, Surrey (this company is a subsidiary of Standard Telephone and Cables which is a subsidiary of International Telephone and Telegraph Corporation); Kelvin Hughes, New North Road, Hainault, Ilford, Essex 1G6 2UR; Redifon Telecommunications Ltd, Broomhill Road, London SW18 4JQ. Some shipping companies employ their own staff. It is advisable to seek advice about employment after training before undertaking the training itself, although there are normally employment opportunities ashore as well as afloat.

Training courses are available from marine radio colleges up and down the country and last from two to three years. The two-year course leads to the Home Office Maritime Radio Communications General Certificate, the minimum qualification. A further 18-week course should provide the Department of Trade Radar Maintenance Certificate. The three-year course leads to both of these plus the Technician Education Council (TEC) Higher Certificate in Radio and Radar (Marine). After 18 months at sea the radio officer may take a further two-term course at college leading to the TEC Higher Diploma in Electronics (Marine).

The cost of these courses falls basically upon the student or his parents, though local education authorities recognise the courses for the purposes of grant and at times some shipping companies sponsor radio cadetships. The radio colleges can offer advice to prospective students, but it is as well to make enquiry of more than one radio college since they do not all offer the full range of courses. In cases of proven hardship The Marine Society may offer loans or grants.

In the highly automated ships of today there is a wide range of electronic and control equipment to be maintained–data loggers, closed circuit television, bridge control of remote machinery, etc. After the training outlined above, inclusive of the TEC Higher Diploma, this work may be carried out by a radio officer who may then be known as the electronics officer. Electronics officers may also be directly recruited by the shipping company from among those ashore who are properly qualified.

Catering officers

Reference to the catering officer has been made already in the section on ratings. The one or two companies operating cruise ships may offer posts as cadet purser or assistant purser and direct enquiry is recommended.

Women at sea

Theoretically women can now train for any of the posts available in the Merchant Navy. In practice few or none train as ratings, and the number of women who have become officers is very few. Most work at sea on deck or in the engine room does not appeal to women. Any young woman who aims to become a Merchant Navy officer will be wise to secure a promise of employment before starting any lengthy course of training.

In cruiseships and on ferries women may find employment as waitresses, stewardesses, nurses and assistant pursers, or even as telephonists, secretaries, shop assistants and hairdressers. But the jobs are very few and such seafarers will have obtained normal shore training for these posts before proceeding to sea.

Merchant Navy Training Courses

Key:

N = teaches navigators; E = teaches engineers; R = teaches radio officers; C = teaches cooks.

Courses & Correspondence Courses–numbers refer to class of certificate; Ex = Extra Master or Extra 1st; En = Endorsements; T = Tugmaster; P = Preparatory; † = Degree Courses.

Aberdeen Aberdeen Technical College, Gallowgate, Aberdeen AB9 1DN (Tel 0224 50366). N Courses 4321 Ex En T. E Courses 321 En. R.C.

Ambleside RMS Wray Castle, Ambleside, Cumbria (tel 096 63 2320). R.

Belfast Northern Ireland Polytechnic, Jordanstown, Newtonabbey, Co. Antrim, N Ireland BT37 0QB (tel 0231 65131). N Courses 4321 Ex. E courses 321 En.E Correspondence 3P 2P.R.

Bristol Brunel Technical College, Ashley Down, Bristol BS7 9BU (tel 0272 41241). N Courses 54321 En T. N Correspondence 543. R.

Cardiff South Glamorgan Insitute of Higher Education, Western Avenue, Cardiff CF5 2YB (tel 0222 561241 or 492121 for Catering). N Courses 54321 En. N Correspondence 5432. E Courses 321 En. R. C.

†UWIST (University of Wales Institute of Science & Technology), King Edward VII Avenue, Cardiff CF1 3NU (tel 0222 42522).

Fleetwood Nautical College, Broadwater, Fleetwood, Lancs FY7 8JZ (tel 039 17 2772).N Courses 321 En. R.

Glasgow Glasgow College of Nautical Studies, 21 Thistle Street, Glasgow G5 9XB (tel 041 429 3201). N Courses 4321 Ex En. E Courses 321 Ex En. E Correspondence 3P 2P. R.

Grimsby Grimsby College of Technology, Nuns Corner, Grimsby, S Humberside (tel 0472 79292). N Courses 43. R.

Hull Hull College of Higher Education, Queens Gardens, Hull HU1 3DH (tel 0482 224121). N Courses 321. N Correspondence 4 3P 2P 1P. E Courses 4321. E Correspondence 2P 1P. R. C.

Leith Leith Nautical College, 24 Milton Road East, Edinburgh EH15 2PP (tel 031 669 8461). N Courses 54321 En. E Courses 321 En. R.

Liverpool Riversdale College of Technology, Riversdale Road, Liverpool L19 3QR (tel 051 427 1227). N Courses 43. E Courses 43. R.

†Liverpool Polytechnic, Byrom Street, Liverpool L3 3AF (tel 051 207 3581). N Courses 21 En. N Correspondence 2P 1P. E Courses 21 En.

Colquitt Technical and Nautical Catering College, Canning Place, Liverpool L1 8BT (tel 051 709 4572). C.

National Sea Training College, Mann Island, Liverpool (tel 01 283 2922 for enquiries). Trains engine-room ratings.

London Merchant Navy College, Greenhithe, Kent DA9 9NY (tel 0322 845050). N Courses 543. N Correspondence 543. R. E cadets

School of Navigation, 100 Minories, Tower Hill, London EC3N 1JY (tel 01 283 1030). N Courses 21 Ex En. N Correspondence. 21 En.

Hackney College, Poplar Centre, Poplar High Street, London E14 0AF (tel 01 987 4205). E Courses 21 Ex En. E Correspondence 2 1P.

Barking Technical College, Dagenham Road, Romford, Essex RM7 0XU (tel 70 66841). R.

London Electronics College, 20 Penywern Road, Earls Court, London SW5 9SU (tel 01 373 8721). R.

London School of Nautical Cookery, 202 Lambeth Road, London SE1 7JW. C.

National Sea Training College, Gravesend, Kent. (tel 01 283 2922 for enquiries). Trains deck & catering ratings.

Lowestoft College of Further Education, Herring Fisher Score, Lowestoft, Suffolk NR32 1XE (tel 0502 3259). N Courses 54321 En T. R.

Manchester College of International Marine Radiotelegraphic Communication, 160-176 Chorlton Road, Manchester M16 7WT (tel 061 226 2047). R.

Plymouth College of Further Education, Portland Square, Plymouth PL4 6DH (tel 0752 21312). N Courses 43. E Courses 432 Part A; also Part B (subject to DES approval). R.

†Plymouth Polytechnic, Drake's Circus, Plymouth PL4 8AA (tel 0752 21312). N Courses 21, HND.

Portsmouth Highbury College of Technology, Cosham, Portsmouth PO6 2SA (tel Cosham 83131). E cadets.

Preston Northern Counties Radio School, 91 Lancaster Road,Preston PR1 2QJ (tel 0772 54364). R.

Southampton †College of Nautical Studies, Warsash, Southampton SO3 62L (tel 048 95 6161). N Courses 54321 En. N Correspondence 21 En.

Southampton College of Technology, East Park Terrace, Southampton SO9 4WW (tel 0703 28523). E Courses 4321 En. E Correspondence 321 En. R. †in conjunction with Southampton College of Higher Education.

South Shields Marine & Technical College, St George's Avenue, South Shields, Tyne & Wear NE34 6ET (tel 0632 560403). N Courses 4321. N Correspondence 43 2P 1P. E Courses 321 Ex En. E Correspondence 3P 2P. R. †in conjunction with Sunderland Polytechnic.
Stornoway Lews Castle College,Stornoway, Isle of Lewis. N cadets.

4 The Merchant Ship and its Organisation

It was different on my last ship.
Any seafarer

Professional seafaring embraces many different companies, many different ships and many different jobs. 'Different ships, different long splices' is a seafaring expression which indicates a lack of uniformity, and the wearing of uniform is a case in point. In some companies uniform is worn; in other companies it is not worn; in many companies only officers wear a uniform; in no company (with the possible exceptions of cruise-ships and ferries) will there be an absolutely standard practice; and no merchant seafarer will wear uniform ashore, except when visiting a school, attending a college, or laying a wreath at the Cenotaph. The Merchant Navy is, after all, a civilian occupation.

Even so, sea life stamps its adherents with a mark both unique and indefinable. And, even though the organisation of ships is changing and crew numbers are decreasing, rank–the distinction between officer and rating–is still something that is clearly understood. In these days officers can outnumber ratings but only in oil-rig supply ships, where crew numbers are as few as seven, is 'messing' (the domestic arrangments) likely to be communal. In the great majority of ships officers and ratings eat separately, have each their own recreation room (for ratings) or smokeroom (for officers) and bar, and sleep in cabins which are on a different deck or in a different part of the ship.

In ships of a traditional type it is still customary to find deck (or navigating), engine-room, catering and radio departments, and each department will have its own chief who is responsible to the master. In the cruise ship a hotel manager rather than a catering officer will be at the head of the catering department, and there will also be a medical officer's department. In the tanker, bulk carrier and container ship general-purpose manning may be adopted, a system under which the ratings are deployed on duties throughout the ship. It is not necessarily the case that each head of department is of equal importance; they complement one another, and all are essential to the efficient running of the ship.

Deck

The master is primarily a navigator and the way to a command is possible only by way of the deck department. Although 'Captain' is used as a form of address

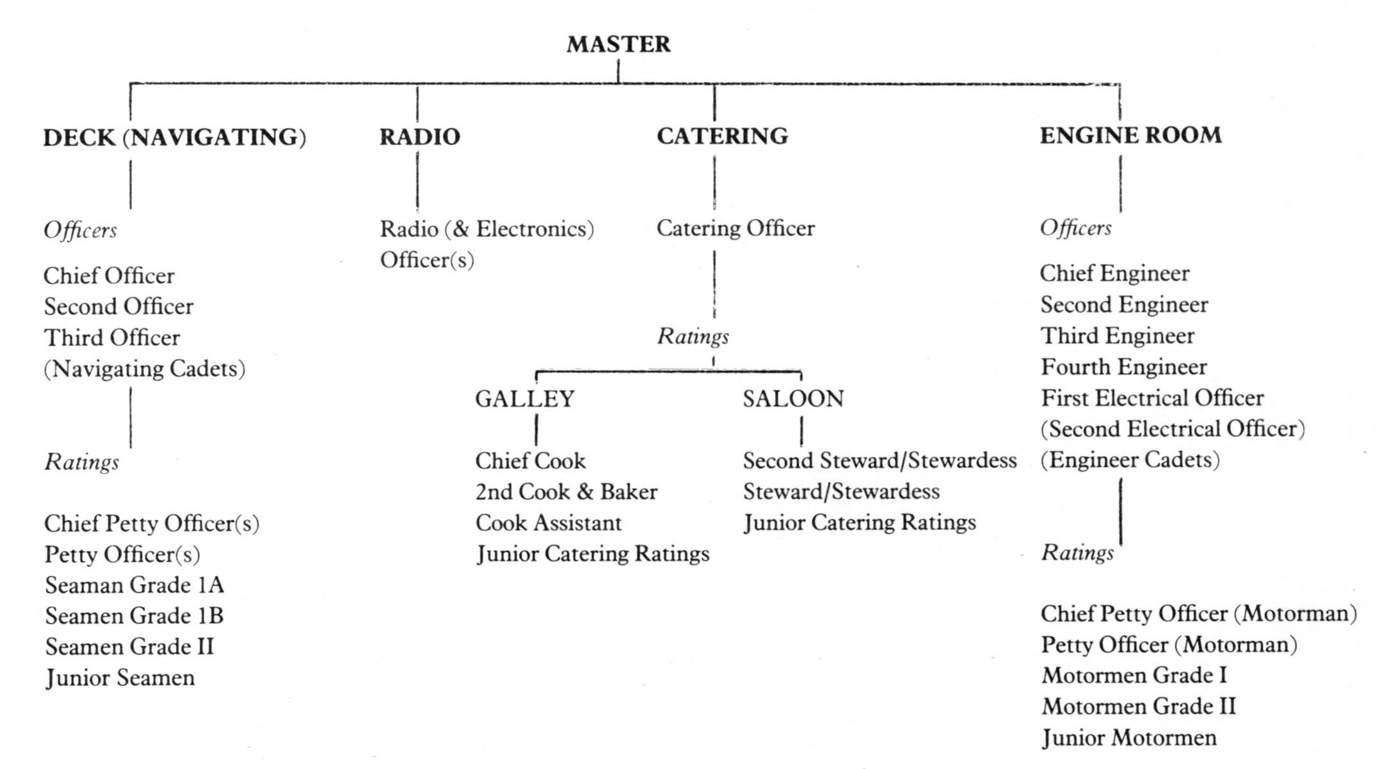

Fig 14 The traditional manning of a merchant ship (with modern terminology)

the master is technically a master mariner and must hold a DoT (Department of Trade) certificate of competency (Deck Officer) Class 1 which states that he has passed an examination and is qualified to act in this capacity. In some ships the master may be described as the ship's manager, and there has been talk of a dual-purpose officer who is trained as both navigator and engineer, but this had not yet come to pass in the United Kingdom.

The chief officer or first officer or mate (the terms are interchangeable) is required to hold a certificate of competency Class 2, and is responsible, under the master, for running the deck department. The stowage of cargo, the ship's stability and the maintenance of the vessel, with the exception of those parts which come under the catering and engine-room departments, are all his direct responsibility except where there are general-purpose ratings, when the chief engineer officer may take responsibility for maintenance. He also supervises the work and studies of the navigating cadets.

Although in many modern ships the nature of the chief officer's job has changed markedly, it has not necessarily become easier. The stowage of cargo in a container ship or tanker is very different from what it is in a traditional cargo-liner, but such ships are larger and faster and, in the loading and discharging of large tankers, liquefied gas carriers and other specialised vessels complex operational procedures have to be followed and completed within a strictly limited period of time. The advent of computerised systems for calculating loading stress in very large ships and other uses of the computer mean that the chief officer of today needs to be far more scientifically oriented than was the chief officer of time past.

The second officer, who will hold at least a Class 3 certificate, normally looks after all charts, lays off courses under the master's supervision and sets the ship's clocks. The third officer, who may have a Class 3 or Class 4 certificate, is usually responsible, among other things, for the maintenance of the ship's life-saving apparatus. There is also a Class 5 certificate which is a watchkeeping qualification aboard vessels under 5,000 gross tons operating in the Baltic Sea or nearer waters. The Department of Trade decrees how many certificated officers are carried aboard any particular vessel and which certificates they should have.

The chief officer normally 'stands' or keeps the 4–8 watch, the second officer keeps the 12–4 watch and the third officer the 8–12 watch. The cadets are generally on day work (that is, keep no night watches) doing a variety of jobs but, depending on the custom of the vessel, with a special responsibility for sounding the fresh water and ballast tanks.

The boatswain (bosun), who is a petty officer or chief petty officer, is directly responsible to the chief officer and takes his orders from him in the morning, subsequently allotting other deck ratings to their jobs. In this sense he may be described as a seagoing foreman! After giving his orders, he works himself, supervising where necessary and bringing his knowledge and experience to bear where it is needed. He also carries out many of the carpenter's duties where no carpenter is carried. The bosun is only required to hold an EDH certificate and his promotion from bosun's mate is a matter for the master or chief officer. At this stage he may be sent on a short management course and, once promoted, he is likely to keep the rank.

Formerly every ship carried a carpenter ('Chippy') but now carpenters are mostly found on refrigerated vessels. The carpenter is a qualified shipwright and will have served his time as an apprentice in a shipyard. The title is a misnomer since his work has little or nothing to do with carpentry. One of his special responsibilities, under the chief officer, is to lower and raise the anchor. Plumbers are normally found only on cruise liners.

A bosun's mate or deck storekeeper has general charge of the deck stores and may stand in for the bosun should that become necessary. Quartermasters may be found nowadays only on cruise-ships or the RFAs: they take the helm (steer the ship) when the ship is not on automatic steering and, in port, stand the gangway watch.

From his entry to the National Sea Training College, the deck rating is described as a junior seaman. After completion of his induction course and two months sea service, if he is then not less than 16½ years of age, he becomes a seaman grade II, provided he has passed the examination for Efficient Deck Hand. If he has not passed the examination he has first to serve four months at sea. He is rated seaman grade 1B when he is 18, provided he has an EDH certificate and has obtained his lifeboatman's certificate. At 20 he can be rated seaman grade 1A.

On most ships the deck rating's or sailor's job is varied and he may find himself doing any form of work from painting the topmast to steering the ship. On an outward voyage in a dry-cargo vessel all cargo running gear will be overhauled, and wires and ropes will be made ready for each port of call.

The sailor must be able to steer, paint, sew, scrub, polish, scrape, splice, drive a winch, keep a lookout, slack away a backspring and do a hundred other jobs. In a cruise-ship an even greater variety of work is open to him, though his hours of work are defined in all ships. Opportunities for overtime vary from ship to ship.

	12–4	**4–8**	**8–12**
am	Middle watch	Morning watch	Forenoon watch
pm	Afternoon watch	Dog watches	First watch
Deck	Second Officer	Chief Officer	Third Officer
Engine	Third Engineer	Second Engineer	Fourth Engineer

Fig 15 Traditional watches in the Merchant Navy

Watches

At sea the deck and engine-room crews are divided into dayworkers and watchkeepers, each working a basic day of eight hours. Dayworkers may start at 7am and work for an hour before the breakfast break at 8am, but otherwise their working day is similar to that ashore. Watchkeepers, however, do their eight hours in two four-hour watches.

Each watch is in the charge of an officer, one on the bridge and another in the engine room, and it is customary for the watches, both am and pm, to be divided among the officers as illustrated.

Despite the need to maintain an organisation which keeps the ship at work all day and every day, the modern seafarer's working week is in line with that ashore. Overtime is paid or extra leave given wherever the seafarer has to offer extra service.

At one time bells were struck to denote the passage of each half-hour of a watch, from one bell to eight bells as the four-hour watch progressed. There was a variation in the second dog watch, from 6pm to 8pm, which began again at 6.30 pm with only one bell, instead of the five bells which would be rung, for example, at 6.30am, but finished with eight bells at 8pm. One bell might also be struck fifteen minutes before a new watch began to warn those coming on watch that the new period of duty was approaching. The quartz crystal watch and the telephone have caused these customs to fall into disuse, except perhaps in cruise-ships where the bells may be struck to 'entertain' the passengers.

In recent years the traditional watchkeeping systems have changed dramatically to meet the requirements of the modern fleet. Six-hour watches are not unknown. Engine-rooms can be unmanned at night. Electronic navigational aids, automatic steering and alarm systems, and more highly developed and automated engine rooms enable a modern vessel to operate with a wide variety of watchkeeping systems, just as it may operate with fewer crew. The primary consideration always must be the safety of the ship.

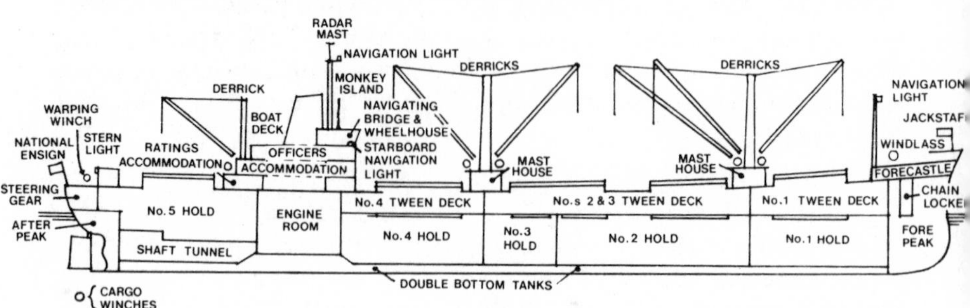

Fig 16 A dry-cargo motorship. The Austin & Pickersgill SD14 15,265 deadweight tons; 9,100 gross tons; 472 feet long, 67 feet in breadth and 29 feet load draft; service speed 15 knots

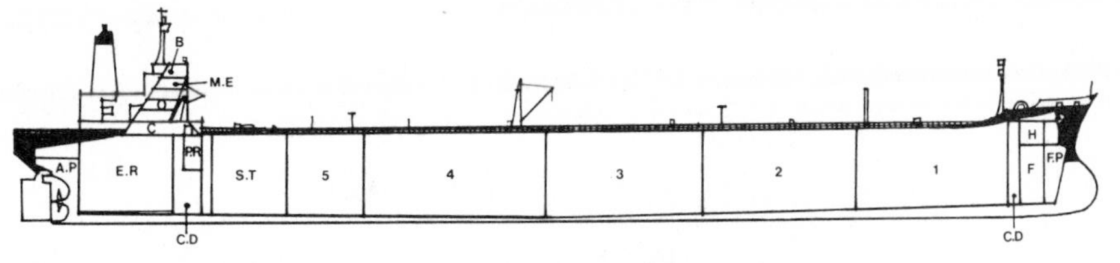

1–5 Cargo tanks
PR Pump room
CD Cofferdams
C Crew accommodation
O Officers' accommodation
ER Engine room
AP After peak for water
F Fuel oil for main engines
H Hold for dry cargo
ST Slop tank for oily water
B Bridge
ME Master's & Chief Engineer's accommodation
FP Forepeak

Fig 17 The main constructional features of a VLCC

Radio

The Radio department often consists of only one man and so the term 'department' may seem out of place. However, the provision of the radio equipment is a legal requirement, and so is the carriage in vessels of more than a certain size of a properly qualified radio officer. In most ships the radio officer ('Sparks') works a shifting watch at sea to align himself to shore time, though his normal working day does not exceed eight hours. During the rest of the day an auto-alarm device responds to telex and emergency calls and rings an alarm bell. On cruise-ships the department will consist of more than one man and a continuous human watch is kept. On all ships the radio is the only contact with the outside world, but radiotelephony often augments radiotelegraphy nowadays and, quite apart from communication by cable, it is common for telephone calls to be made to and from modern ships, the radio linking the ship to a landline. Many of the business messages which the radio officer sends and receives are concerned with the arrival of the vessel and the cargo she is to load. He also receives regular weather information.

In an age of electronic aids the radio department is closely associated with the navigation of the vessel, and it is becoming increasingly common for the radio officer to be trained as an electronics officer as well, taking responsibility for the servicing and maintenance at sea of a variety of electronic equipment.

Engine room

The modern ship's propulsive unit, whether steam turbine or diesel engine, is run on oil, and the engine-room department comprises a team of engineer

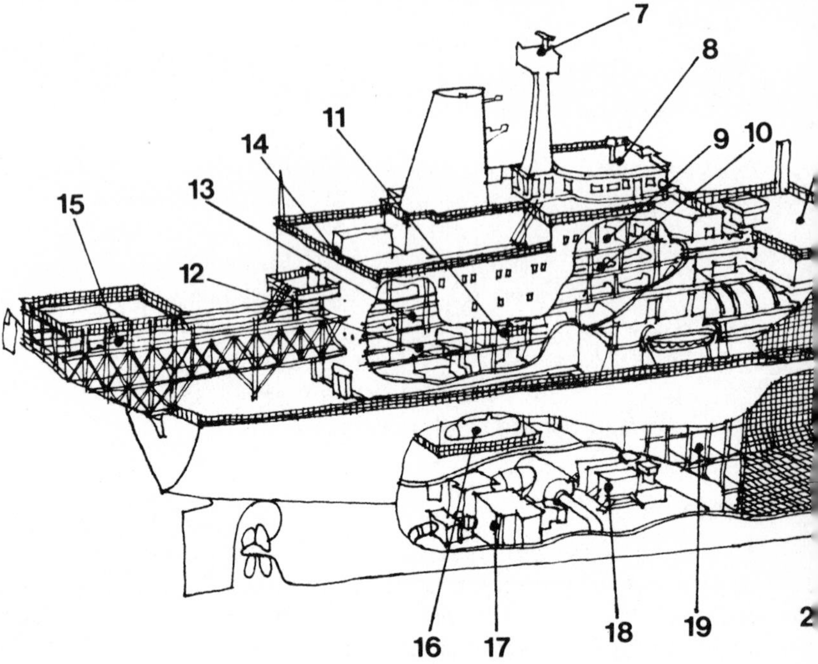

Key

1 Bulbous bow
2 Cargo tank vent risers
3 Deck floodlight
4 Deck cranes
5 Discharge pipelines
6 Gas compressor house
7 Radar scanner
8 Wheelhouse
9 Master's accommodation
10 Officers' accommodation
11 Crew messroom
12 Galley
13 Crew accommodation
14 Swimming pool
15 Stern loading pipelines
16 Main boiler

Fig 18 A modern LNG carrier

officers and ratings controlled by the chief engineer officer who ranks with but immediately after the master.

The main engine is but one part of thework of the engine-room staff. Every service that is taken for granted in homes ashore has to come from the engine room of a seagoing vessel: electric light, heat, running water and refrigeration.

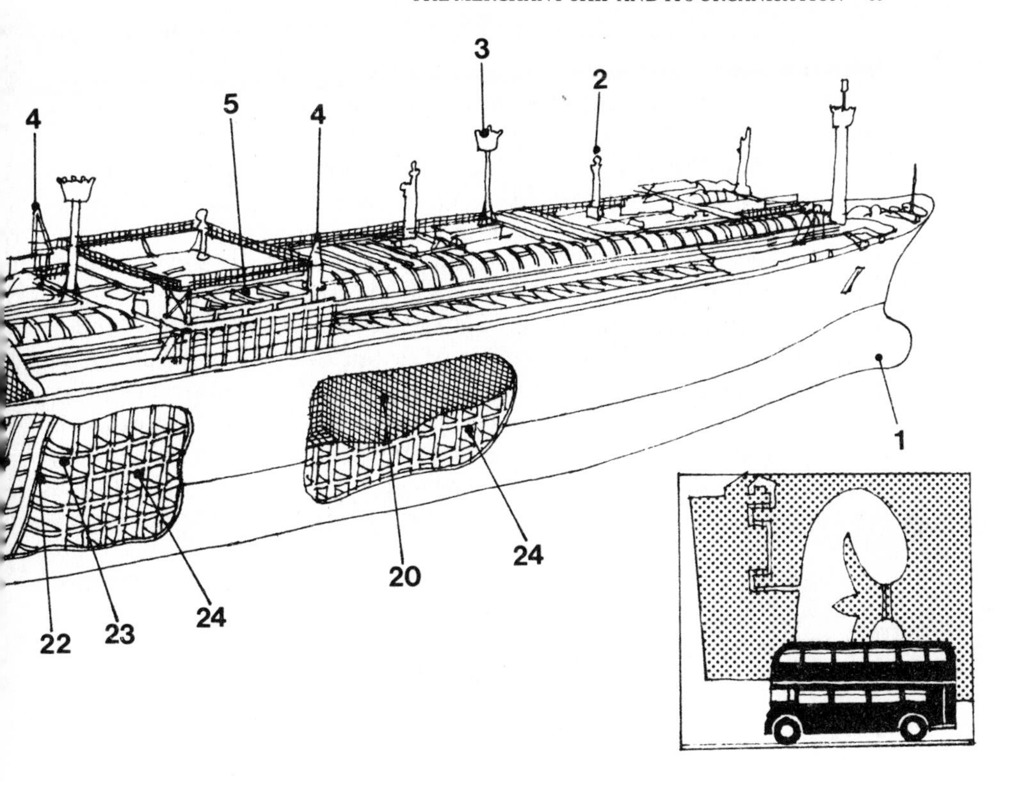

17 Main propulsion unit
18 Diesel generators
19 Oil fuel bunker tank
20 Cargo compartments
21 Insulation layers comprising:
 (a) Wood grounds and fibre glass
 (b) Balsa wood
 (c) Stainless steel membrane
22 Inner hull longitudinal bulkhead
23 Transverse bulkhead
24 Wing ballast tanks

Nowadays it is common to find an engine room fully automated and controlled from an air-conditioned control room insulated against noise. As indicated above, this control room may be unmanned at night with automatic alarms calling attention to anything that goes wrong. Under these conditions the engineers become service engineers rather than watchkeepers.

In vessels with more than 3,000 kilowatts registered power, and trading in other than near-continental waters, the chief engineer officer must hold a Class I certificate of competency from the Department of Trade and his second engineer is required to hold a Class 2 certificate. There must also be on board two other engineer officers with at least the Class 4 certificate. The second engineer keeps the 4–8 watch and is also responsible for the general maintenance of the engine room.The third engineer keeps the 12–4 watch and where an electrical officer is not carried usually maintains the ship's electrical equipment. The fourth engineer keeps the 8–12 watch and is often responsible for overhauling the pumps and maintaining the boilers when the ship is in port. If a fifth engineer (perhaps uncertificated) is carried he will normally spend part of his watch with the second engineer and, in suitable weather, may be on day work on deck engaged in minor repair work or in overhauling winches. Should the ship be carrying refrigerated cargo and not have a refrigerating engineer, the fifth engineer may be on night duty keeping a two-hourly log of temperatures and pressures. Engineer cadets are generally employed on day work.

One or more electrical officers ('Lecky') may be carried on certain ships and their work may take them anywhere on the ship. Although some marine engineering colleges offer courses for electrical officers there are no cadetships in this field. Such work is open to any qualified electrician. A ship which specialises in refrigerated cargo will normally carry three refrigeration engineers who, as watchkeepers, keep a constant eye on the all-important temperatures and pressure gauges.

The old terms 'fireman' and 'greaser' for the engine-room rating have now been superseded, at least officially, by 'motorman'. The junior motorman embarks upon a short pre-sea training course and is upgraded to motorman grade II after nine months' sea service; anyone entering the industry above the age of 19 can be automatically graded motorman grade II if he can produce evidence of mechanical skill or experience. An ex-trainee entrant who is at least 18 and who has served in a lower capacity for at least a year can be upgraded to motorman grade I provided he possesses a Merchant Navy Training Board certificate and a lifeboatman's certificate. Adult entrants have to be at least 19½ with a minimum of six months' sea service. The motorman grade I can be promoted to petty officer (motorman) if he is over 21 and has served at least two years in the former capacity.

Motormen have to see that burner nozzles remain clean and that the furnaces are not being clogged with carbon from the burning oil fuel. They also have to regulate the fuel pump pressure and oil temperatures so as to obtain efficient combustion without smoke from the funnel. The careless motorman, like the careless helmsman when the ship is not on automatic steering, is readily detected and the nature of the smoke tells the knowledgeable observer whether

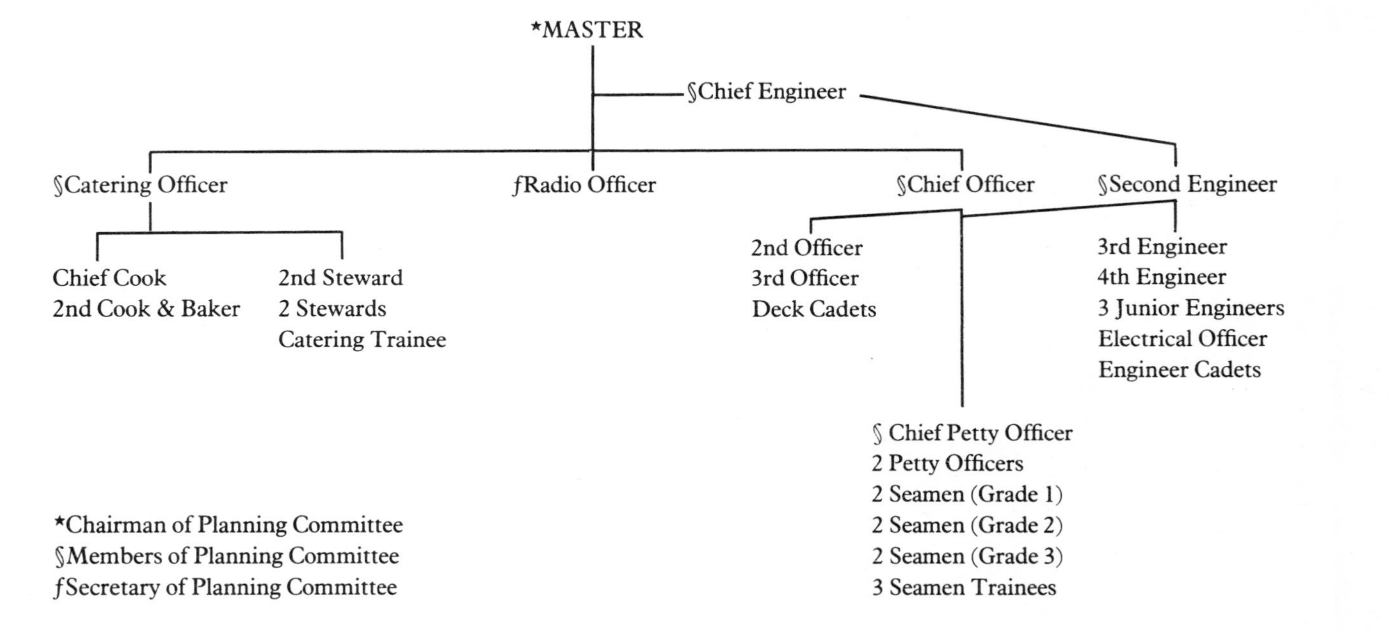

Fig 19 The organisation of a tanker with general purpose crew

Note: The organisation of a container ship is similar but there is sometimes a change of nomenclature, e.g. the Chief Officer becomes First Officer (N), where N = navigation; and the Catering Officer becomes Second Officer (Catering) to indicate that he is of equivalent rank to the Second Officer (N), the Second Officer (Radio) (i.e. the Radio Officer) and the Second Officer (E) (i.e. the Third Engineer), the Second Engineer having become First Officer (E) to indicate his parity with the First Officer (N).

too much oil or too much air is the cause of the trouble. In conventionally manned ships there are usually three watchkeeping motormen, one to a watch. In highly automated ships engine-room ratings may spend most of their time on day work doing maintenance jobs.

The traditional name for the bosun's counterpart in the engine room is the donkeyman (because he was originally responsible for the donkey engine, a small engine which hauled in the cable, worked the derrick, etc). Donkeymen are petty officers and might maintain the same sea watches as the officers, their tasks including the lubrication of machinery and the pumping out of the bilges. When a ship is in port it is customary for two of the donkeymen to take 12 hour shifts in the engine room, maintaining steam and attending to pumps, while the third donkeyman is on deck attending to the lubrication of winches. The rota is changed at each port so that overtime is shared evenly. In addition, there may also be an engine-room storekeeper ('Stores') of petty officer rank.

In tankers the pumpman ranks as a petty officer. At sea he works directly under the chief engineer, maintaining cargo pumps, deck valves and cargo pipelines, but in port, while the ship is loading or discharging cargo, he works under the direction of the chief officer.

Some ships carry engine-room mechanics who have taken a special course ashore before being rated for this higher grade work. With anticipated developments in equipment and control systems it may be that engineering petty officers trained in this way will play an increasingly important part aboard ship. It is possible to reach certificated rank by way of this scheme.

General purpose manning

Aboard some vessels general-purpose or GP ratings take the place of the motormen and the sailors of traditionally manned ships. These are trained to carry out maintenance and watchkeeping duties either in the engine room or on deck, and as members of a combined work force are employed as considered necessary by the ship's planning committee or management team.

The planning committee or team in a GP-manned ship usually comprises the master (as chairman), the chief engineer, the chief officer, the second engineer, the catering officer (otherwise purser/chief steward) and the chief petty officer, the radio officer acting as secretary. The committee meets formally once a week, or as otherwise agreed, to establish long term requirements for the work force, daily meetings to up-date these requirements being held if conditions necessitate them.

An advantage claimed for such manning is that in this way ships can be operated more efficiently, with ratings working where the demand is greatest. Thus during bad weather, when deck maintenance is not possible, the work force might be employed in the engine-room, which is at least under cover. As well as in maintenance, watchkeeping and manual steering (when the latter proves necessary), GP ratings are employed in cargo work and mooring operations. The chief petty officer is in charge of this work force. In such ships GP petty officers are capable of performing the duties of carpenter, boatswain, donkeyman and, in the case of tankers, pumpman.

IDF or inter-departmental flexibility is a variation of the GP scheme in which the original departmental structure is retained but where, by agreement, a member of one department may work in another department if required to do so.

Catering

On going to sea the junior catering rating will find that in most companies he is attached either to the saloon section or to the galley section of the catering department. In the saloon section he will be expected to maintain the service pantry in good order and the cleanliness of the crockery will be an important part of his duties. Under the supervision of the second steward he may also have the work of looking after officers' cabins. He can make some of these duties more attractive by learning the art of salad preparation and taking a lively interest in saloon service as a *commis* waiter.

The junior catering rating on galley duties will have to maintain cookery utensils in a clean condition and in many cases is expected to prepare potatoes and other vegetables for the cook. He should understudy the cooks, since this is an opportunity to learn a useful craft which will stand him in good stead. A foreign-going ship must carry a cook with a certificate of competency as ship's cook.

An ambitious young man will want to serve for a period in both sections of the catering department in order to accept promotion when the opportunity occurs. Promotion is normally to steward at the age of 18.

The duties of a steward cover cabin work, the cleaning of public rooms and alleyways, and the service of food and drink. The steward will know how to lay up and attend at table and how to make beds and bunks; he should be able to carry out his duties in such a manner that the department functions like a well-run household.

The second steward, who must have followed a second steward's course and be in possession of a lifeboatman's certificate, is the leading steward of the department and often ranks as a petty officer. His duties include the care of the master's and chief engineer's suites; he exercises supervision over the other stewards and junior catering ratings under the direction of the catering officer; and he must be competent to deal with the supply of stores and linen.

The second cook, or second cook and baker, carries out his duties under the supervision of the chief cook, and his duties include the preparation and cooking of food. A second cook should be encouraged to make bread and pastries so that he may qualify for promotion. As his rating implies, the second cook and baker makes bread and pastries, though nowadays some ships carry bread and cake deep-frozen for the round trip. Some other food, too, may be carried deep-frozen or prepared.

The chief cook has to ensure that all food is prepared correctly and served presentably. He must be a competent cook, baker and butcher and should be ready to give the benefit of his own experience to his assistants. If he wishes to be considered for further promotion he must understudy the catering officer. In cruise-liners, the chef runs a large staff of his own and among his duties is included the planning of menus. In all cases the chief cook or chef should have a knowledge of provision scales and be able to handle cold-room stocks to the satisfaction of the catering officer. In certain companies his status is above that of a petty officer.

As head of a department the catering officer is responsible to the master for matters affecting his department. His duties embrace the entire catering arrangements on board, including purchases and control. He is responsible for the cleanliness of the officers' accommodation, the deployment of staff, and the submission of the various records and forms required by the company and port officials. He is responsible for the administration of the bond and slop chest, and is required by many companies to maintain stock records, re-order levels, etc, of general stores. He is normally responsible to the master for the treatment of minor ailments and the issue of medicines. (A doctor is carried aboard ship only where the ship's complement numbers one hundred or more). The catering officer must hold a Catering Officer's certificate, which incorporates the DoT certificate for the Ship Captain's Medical Course.

The hours of work in the catering department of many cargo ships and tankers are between 6am and 7pm with a 'break' period, apart from meal breaks, of some two or three hours in the afternoon. Overtime is paid wherever it is worked.

Purser's department

In the modern cruise-liner what used to be called the purser's department may now be called the hotel-manager's department. In either case the functions of the head of department combine those of hotel manager, travel agent, entertainments officer and even bank manager. In such ships the staff in this department are responsible for all matters concerning the welfare, comfort and entertainment of passengers, for the keeping of accounts (possibly including the payment of crew wages), for complying with customs and immigration formalities and for much else. The diagram, which illustrates the organisation of a large cruise-liner, indicates the specialised staff who will work under the hotel manager but this type of organisation is now found in very few ships.

Women at sea

All jobs open to men at sea are open to women–in theory. In fact, few women choose to attempt most of these jobs. In recent years some companies have taken on young women as navigating and engineer cadets, and a few have served as radio officers. Any young woman who is attracted to such a career will be wise to secure a promise of employment before embarking upon any lengthy course of training.

Traditionally, women have served at sea as stewardesses in ships carrying passengers. Almost invariably they have trained ashore and/or had industrial experience ashore before going to sea after the age of 21. From now on it may become more common for women to work as stewardesses and cooks aboard other types of vessel.

Apart from the work indicated above, the posts in which women of the right age, qualifications and experience may secure employment at sea include those of nursing sister, children's hostess, nursery stewardess, assistant purser, secretary, telephonist, hairdresser, laundress, shop assistant and swimming-pool attendant. Such jobs, if available at all, will be available only on ships carrying passengers, and the total number of many of these jobs in the entire Merchant Navy is under twenty.

In most deep sea ships these days one or more wives will be found on board travelling with their husbands. Some companies even allow children to accompany seafarers too. The Marine Society will offer advice on children's education, and its general facilities are available to wives accompanying their husbands.

Safety

More is done by shipping companies today than was the practice in days gone by to ensure that the new recruit to a ship is properly introduced to his shipmates, his job and the onboard organisation. The Merchant Navy Training Board produces induction guidance and offers short training courses in personnel management and ship management.

In no area is proper induction to the organisation of a merchant ship more important than in that of safety. A Code of Safe Working Practices on Board Ship has been agreed and every ship carries a copy. A condensed version of the code entitled Personal Safety on Ships is distributed to every seafarer. The problem, of course, is to persuade everyone to implement the Code. It is better to be safe than sorry.

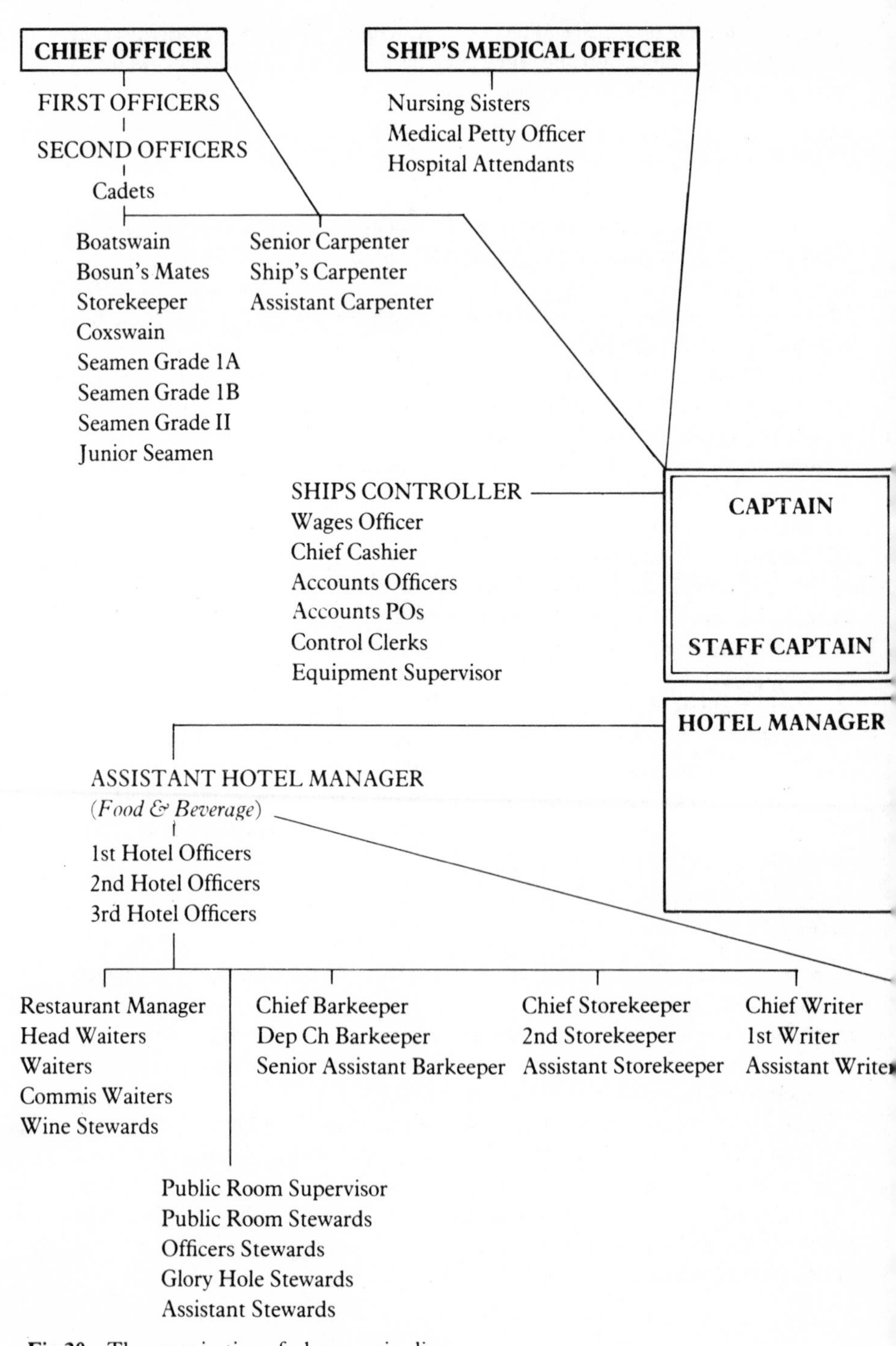

Fig 20 The organisation of a large cruise-liner

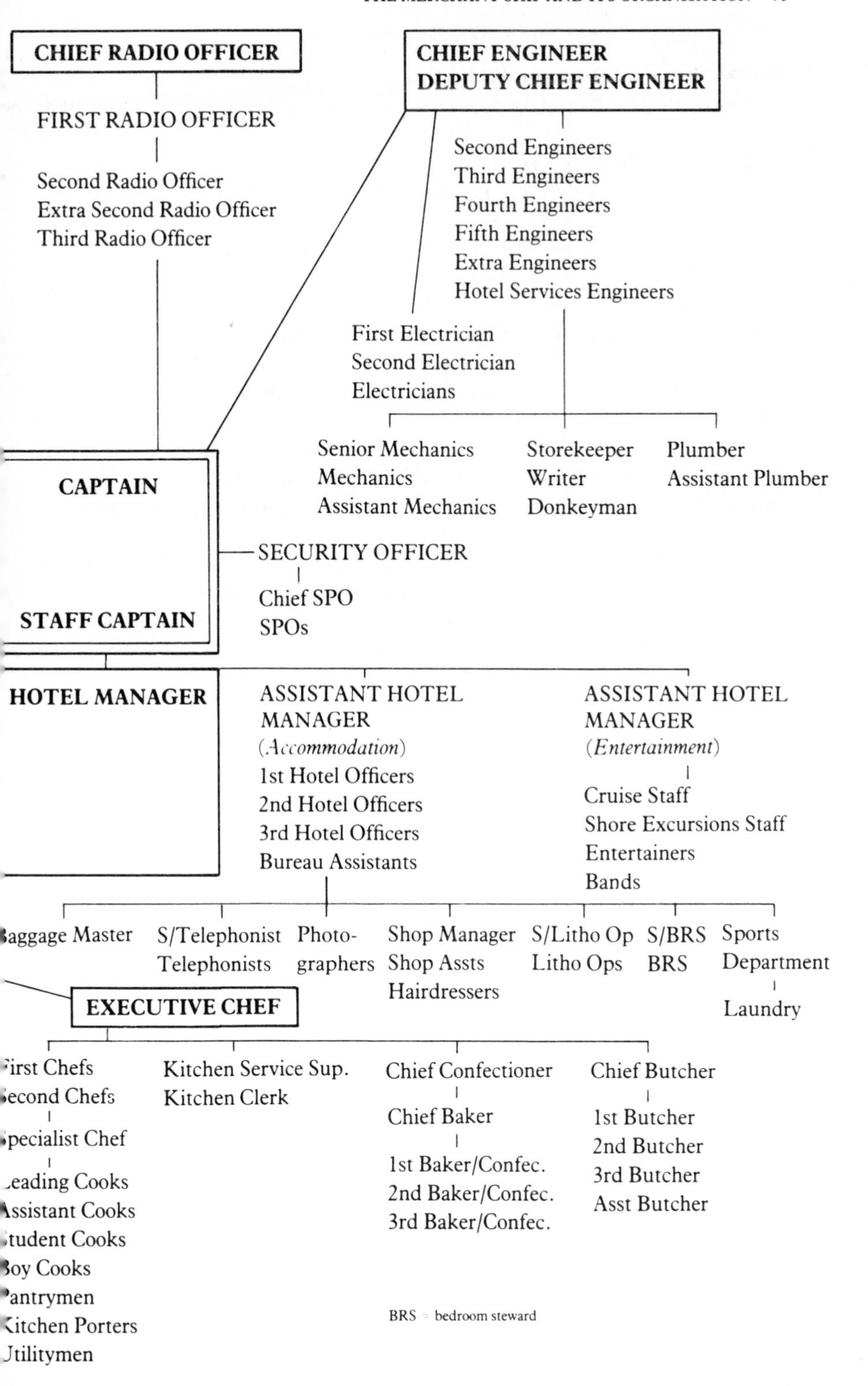

BRS = bedroom steward

Leisure time

Aboard ship the food is almost invariably good and there is plenty of it. On warm-weather runs modern ships are fully air-conditioned, and each crew member has his own cabin and probably his own washing and toilet facilities. In newer ships he may well sleep in a double bed; or a double room will be made available when he is accompanied by his wife. Senior officers may have an office and a lounge (day-room) as well as a bedroom and bathroom. All of these will be comfortably furnished and well equipped. A personal cassette-player and radio may add to the pleasures of life.

Communal accommodation includes a lounge (smoke-room or recreation room) and bar, and possibly a hobbies workshop, a mini-gym or a quiet room. Communal facilities normally include a library regularly exchanged by The Marine Society, a small swimming pool, one or more feature films a week and/or closed-circuit television at sea and normal television in port. Equipment for indoor games is provided but the facilities for taking exercise out doors are often inadequate. In a growing number of ships a Ship's Company Committee makes itself responsible for organising the ship's social life in so far as it requires organisation.

Communal activities are strictly limited by the small size of the modern ship's crew. People are always on duty and it may be difficult to arrange even a game of cards. The seafarer needs to be able to entertain himself, and it is worth pursuing a hobby or continuing one's education. In these spheres The Marine Society offers advice and help.

5 Documents, Pay and Discipline

More days, more dollars.
Seaman's saying

No person may lawfully supply seamen to any ship at a port in the United Kingdom without holding a licence issued by the Department of Trade. The present practice is to restrict the issue of licences to named officials of the General Council of British Shipping, acting on behalf of the Merchant Navy Establishment Administration, and to the consular officials of certain Scandinavian governments. The licences are not issued to commercially operated employment agencies supplying staff for profit. The overall effect of this is that the majority of men are supplied to United Kingdom ships, without charge to the men themselves, by the GCBS.

Documents

Regulations made under Sections 70 and 71 of the Merchant Shipping Act 1970 require certain persons to apply for either or both of two important documents, namely a British Seaman's Card (BSC) and a discharge book. These are issued on personal application to United Kingdom Mercantile Marine Offices on production of proof that an applicant for a BSC is a British seaman with the right of abode in the United Kingdom, and an applicant for a discharge book is employed or has the offer of employment on a United Kingdom registered ship.

A BSC is an identity document, for the purpose of the International Labour Organisation Seafarers' Identity Documents Convention 1958, containing personal details including a photograph of the holder. It is initially valid for five years and may be revalidated for a further five years. In countries which are signatories to the Convention a BSC is accepted instead of a passport when the holder wishes to go ashore although he may also be required to carry other documents such as a visa. A holder of a BSC normally retains it in his possession during its period of validity but he must surrender it if he ceases to be a seaman.

The discharge book, which also contains personal details and a photograph of the holder, is issued to a British national or an alien serving on a United Kingdom registered ship. It contains spaces for records of voyages on such ships and also for a record of leave and certain non-sea-going service. A discharge book is taken from the holder when he signs on a ship and it is returned to him on discharge by the master. The Secretary of State for Trade may also withdraw a discharge book either permanently or for a specified period if the holder has been dismissed from his ship because of a breach of the National Maritime Board Code of Conduct for the Merchant Navy (see paragraphs relating to Merchant Navy discipline).

It is also advisable to be in possession of a valid passport as difficulties are sometimes encountered when travelling to or through countries which are not signatories to the above mentioned Seafarers' Identity Documents Convention or when travelling via an inland airport of a signatory country.

In addition to the documents mentioned, every seaman should have in his possession a national insurance number card, a form from the Merchant Navy Establishment Administration confirming his eligibility for employment and, if proceeding to countries requiring vaccination, a valid vaccination certificate. A medical examination before shipment is usual and, in the case of those under 18 years of age, is required by law.

Superintendents, consuls and shipping masters are available to give information about official requirements and to assist seamen in difficulty, particularly overseas. Seamen are strongly advised to take great care of their documents as loss can cause inconvenience and perhaps the expense of obtaining replacements.

Wherever the Merchant Navy Establishment Administration supplies seafarers they have to join an appropriate union or association, the National Union of Seamen in the case of ratings, the Merchant Navy and Airline Officers Association in the case of navigating and engineer cadets, and the Radio and Electronic Officers Association in the case of radio officers.

Engagement and discharge

The provisions of the Merchant Shipping Act 1894 which required the engagement and discharge of seamen on United Kingdom registered ships to be undertaken in the presence of a Mercantile Marine Office Superintendent were repealed by the Merchant Shipping Act 1970 and so this is no longer a legal requirement. Now the superintendent's main responsibility is to ensure that broadly similar tasks are carried out by the ship's captain, or his representative, acting on behalf of the shipowning employer. The superintendent therefore visits ships on an *ad hoc* basis only, except in certain instances where his presence on board is requested by a seafarer or shipmaster.

The employer of a seaman must give notice of his intention to employ him under a crew agreement to either a Mercantile Marine Office Superintendent in the United Kingdom, British Consul in a foreign country or a Shipping

Master in a Commonwealth Country or Dependent Territory. At a seaman's engagement or signing on the master or other person authorised by the employer will check that his documents, including his certificates of competency where these are possessed, are in order, ask if he wishes to make an allotment, and, if necessary, explain any provisions of the crew agreement. A seaman may not be discharged at a port outside the United Kingdom without the consent of a proper officer (British Consul or Shipping Master), and the master is required to notify the proper officer of the name and place of discharge of any seaman. Similar requirements exist for the discharge of any seaman at United Kingdom ports. On discharge seamen sign off the crew agreement and their signature is witnessed by the master by the person otherwise authorised by the employer.

The crew agreement

The employment of any seaman as a member of a ship's crew is formalised by the signing of the crew agreement, the form and provisions of which must be approved by the Department of Trade. The crew agreement is a contract of employment between the employing company, formally represented by the master, and the individual seaman. Among the items entered in the crew agreement alongside the seaman's signature are: details of his next-of-kin, his rank or rating, the date when he started employment on board and his rate of wages. These details also form part of the list of crew of a ship which is required for reasons of safety.

The minimum terms and conditions of a seafarer's employment, including wages, overtime and leave entitlements, are established by the decisions of the National Maritime Board, a joint organisation of shipowners and seafarers' trade union representatives. National Maritime Board terms and conditions of employment are incorporated in the crew agreement by means of a standard contractual clause and a summary of National Maritime Board agreements is carried on each ship and may be referred to by any member of the crew. Some of the more important clauses in the crew agreement are those describing the destination, duration of the voyage, the period of service after which a seaman may give notice to terminate the agreement and the circumstances under which the agreement may be terminated.

The agreement embraces clauses which are mutually agreed, clauses which impose obligations on the seafarer and clauses to which the employer must be bound. Clauses of the first type include a stipulation that the seaman will be employed, serving in a stated capacity, eg able seaman, in return for an agreed rate of pay. Conversely both parties agree that if the seaman fails to work through wilful neglect he shall not be entitled to be paid for the period of his absence from duty. The second category of clauses is exemplified by the seaman's undertaking to be punctual, to protect ship's property and to keep his accommodation clean and tidy. An illustration of the clauses binding the employer is one in which the shipowner undertakes to compensate the seafarer should he be discharged other than in accordance with the terms of the crew agreement.

An important feature of the agreement is that it provides for a deduction to be made from the wages due to a seaman for a breach by him of certain obligations under the agreement. The deduction is limited to £50 by Regulations made under the 1970 Merchant Shipping Act and the seaman may appeal to the master or his employer against the deduction.

Every ship must carry a copy of the crew agreement. In addition a copy of the agreement, or extracts from it containing the terms thereof applicable to any or all of the seamen employed on board, must be displayed in some conspicuous place for any seaman to read. A seaman is also entitled to be supplied, on demand, with a copy of the crew agreement and he is entitled to have made available to him a copy of any document referred to in the agreement.

Cash advances

At sea wages are not normally paid weekly or monthly although some employers do operate a monthly computer pay-roll system. A seaman's earnings accumulate and must be paid to him in full when he is discharged from the ship except that, where it is not practicable to pay the whole of the sum due at the time of discharge, not less than £50 nor less than one quarter of the amount due shall be paid on discharge and the balance within seven days. If a seaman has a dispute with his employer about his wages, he may, if the employer agrees, submit the dispute to a Mercantile Marine Office Superintendent or proper officer (see above) for a decision.

In the meantime he may require cash to satisfy his immediate personal needs and such requirement is met by the cash advance. In the case of a seaman taking up employment on board ship the National Maritime Board has recommended: 'Except in the case of men leaving shore employment and coming back to sea, advance notes should be restricted to one week's advance, two weeks if an allotment is made'. Another NMB recommendation deals with cash advances which may be made during the course of a voyage. A seaman may obtain a cash advance provided that (i) allotments and statutory deductions can be met from the remaining balance of wages, and (ii) there is no evidence that the seaman concerned is likely to inconvenience the ship if the advance is made.

Seamen should consider how much money they have in the ship and not ask for money not yet earned. Money granted abroad is usually paid out in the local currency and is charged at the prevailing rate of exchange.

Allotments

Arrangements may be made whereby certain agreed sums of money can be paid regularly on the seaman's behalf, to a person of his choosing, while he is away at sea. An allotment, as it is called, may be paid, by agreement, at weekly, fortnightly or monthly intervals. A National Maritime Board agreement stipulates that the total amount allotted shall not exceed 90 per cent of the seaman's wages–as distinct from earnings–after allowance has been made for statutory deductions. A second monthly allotment may be made to a bank but this too is included within the 90 per cent embargo.

The allotment note facilitates saving and is a safeguard against robbery or loss at the end of a voyage. The seaman should send his copy of the allotment note to the person or bank in whose favour the allotment is made and this gives whoever it may be the right to receive the amount stated by presenting or posting the note to the shipowner or agent mentioned thereon whenever payment is due.

Shore leave

The shorter the period a ship stops in port the less opportunity there is for seafarers to go ashore. Shore leave is granted at the discretion of the captain and his decision is usually issued as a written notice which is normally placed near the ship's gangway. The notice customarily states when shore leave begins and ends. A ship continues to work in port and unless clearly defined arrangements have been made shore leave should not be taken during working hours. Every effort should be made to be back on board ship before shore leave ends. Should he fail to return, the seaman may find that the ship has sailed or that a substitute has been engaged to replace him. In either case his employment with the ship may be terminated and arrangements will have to be made for his eventual return to the United Kingdom. A seaman left behind in this way should report to the ship's agent, the British consul or the local police. If his late return to the ship has been occasioned through no fault of his own, he should try to obtain written testimony to this effect if at all possible. Failure to demonstrate that his delayed return was not brought about by his own carelessness could make it possible for his employer to claim special damages of up to £100 from him.

The employer of a seaman who is left behind in any place outside of the United Kingdom is responsible for his relief, maintenance and repatriation to the United Kingdom. The seaman's employer is thus liable for the costs of repatriation as well as many of the incidental expenses which may include medical treatment, clothing and food and lodging. An employer is liable to repatriate a seaman even if he has deserted from his ship but the obligation is limited to a period of three months after the seaman was left behind and may also cease if the seaman refuses to co-operate with any reasonable arrangements made by his employer for his return. The balance of wages due to a seaman left behind abroad, if any, will be paid to him, subject to the provisions of the Merchant Shipping Act 1970 and the Repatriation Regulations.

Desertion abroad was once commonplace and many families in Australia and New Zealand trace their ancestry to a seaman who 'jumped ship'. Today things are very different and apart from any legal remedies available to the master, the governments of these and other countries take a highly unfavourable view of illegal immigrants. The only advice that can be given to the would-be deserter is 'Don't'.

Merchant Navy discipline

It has been said above that the Merchant Navy is a civilian service and that such discipline as the merchant seafarer endures is largely imposed upon the ship by the sea itself. While this is undoubtedly true, there is rather more to it than that. Because a ship at sea is beyond the immediate influence of the law, there is need for an effective framework of do's and don'ts.

Serious misconduct by both officers and ratings and the punishment imposed on them is entered in the official log book, hence the term 'logging'. Prior to 1 January1973 if a man was logged too often or on too serious a matter a master would stamp DR (decline to report) in the man's discharge book where he was required to comment on ability and conduct. The usual comment was VG (very good), and DR gave the next master some idea of what the last one thought of a particular man which thus lessened his chances of employment. A master had (and still has on non-federated ships) the power to impose a fine on a rating guilty of misconduct. An officer was exempt from such fines but he could be dismissed from his ship and perhaps lose his certificate of competency. From 1st January 1973 the columns for ability and conduct were omitted from the seaman's discharge book and instead the master was required to submit a report on each rating to the predecessor the General Council of British Shipping. Although hailed as a progressive step, the submission of such reports did not please all ratings.

In January 1979 the National Maritime Board adopted new disciplinary procedures based on the recommendations and the Code of Conduct in the Report of the Working Group on Discipline in the Merchant Navy. The Code clarifies the concept of shipboard discipline and makes far-sweeping changes in the machinery to deal with offences. The master no longer wields the magisterial authority of the past; serious matters which result in a rating or officer being dismissed from a ship are now referred to a shore-based disciplinary committee. The offender retains any right to appeal to an industrial tribunal against unfair dismissal and any such appeal takes precedence over a disciplinary committee hearing.

If a ship is to operate safely and efficiently orders must be given and obeyed, and the first direction in the Code of Conduct deals particularly with emergencies. In any emergency orders must be obeyed immediately and unquestioningly. Failure to comply will be treated as a serious breach of the Code and may result in dismissal from the ship and perhaps the Merchant Navy, as well as prosecution under the Merchant Shipping Acts.

Seafarers, however, are not always working in conditions of emergency. They spend their leisure hours as well as their working hours on board ship and with the same people for company. This can sometimes lead to tension and misconduct, and some misconduct can lead to a state of emergency–absence from a place of duty, for example. This contingency apart, the Code of Conduct is concerned with setting out some broad general rules for everyday behaviour.

First comes the need for *punctuality*. Second comes a warning against taking *drugs* of any description on board. Third is a warning to follow the ship's rules on *drink* and not to abuse the privileges which exist. Fourth, seafarers are told that they should not bring *unauthorised persons* on board, nor, fifthly, *offensive weapons*. The sixth rule warns against *smoking in prohibited areas*. Seventh, every member of the crew is told to carry out his *duties* efficiently and to the best of his ability, and to ask if he is in any doubt as to what these duties are. Eighth, the seafarer is asked to treat *accommodation* with respect. Lastly, he is warned against *anti-social behaviour*.

All this is simple commonsense. Minor breaches of the Code of Conduct are dealt with by informal or formal warnings or by a written reprimand, formal warnings and written reprimands by the master being recorded in the ship's official logbook.

More serious misconduct would include assault, wilful damage, theft, possession of offensive weapons, wilful failure to perform duty, the unlawful possession or distribution of drugs, conduct endangering the ship or persons on board, combination with others to impede the progress of the voyage, disobedience of orders relating to safety, failure to be on duty where safety is prejudiced, incapacity through drink or drugs, smoking or using naked lights in dangerous places, intimidation of others, ill behaviour likely to affect the safety or efficient working of the ship or the social well-being of others on board, and admitting unauthorised persons on board so that they sail with the ship.

The commission of any of these acts will invariably be referred to the master and may lead to dismissal from the ship and perhaps prosecution in a court of law. The master has to deal with cases referred to him with the minimum of delay. The seafarer may call witnesses on his own behalf. If, after investigation, the master decides that the offence merits dismissal, the matter has to be reported to a shore-based Disciplinary Committee. If the master decides that the continued presence of the offender on board would be detrimental to the efficient and safe running of the ship or to the maintenance of harmonious personal relations on board, he may arrange for dismissal to take place at the next port of call for repatriation to the United Kingdom. All this must be entered in the official log, a copy given to the seafarer and receipt of this by the seafarer must be acknowledged.

On receipt of a report of dismissal for breach of the Code of Conduct, a shore-based Disciplinary Committee, constituted in a manner agreed by the Secretary of State for Trade, will consider the evidence and make appropriate recommendations concerning the seafarer's future employment in the shipping industry. The seafarer has the right to be accompanied by a friend, who may advise him and speak on his behalf, whenever an alleged breach of the Code is being considered against him.

In the event of dismissal a seafarer may contact an official of the appropriate seafarers' organisation who may take up the matter with an appropriate manager of the shipping company concerned. In such event the two representatives shall meet within five days to discuss the issue.

Nothing in the Code of Conduct is to be read as negating any seafarer's right to bring an unfair dismissal claim before an Industrial Tribunal as provided in the Employment Protection (Consolidation) Act, 1978. Failure to contact a seafarers' organisation or an Industrial Tribunal, or to take a case to an Industrial Tribunal should the union and employer representatives declare his dismissal fair, will be taken as *prima facie* evidence that the seafarer accepts his dismissal as fair and of his willingness to abide by the decision of a shore-based Disciplinary Committee as to eventual disciplinary action.

Account of wages

Sooner or later every voyage comes to an end and the seaman receives the balance of his wages. Before paying off he is given an account of wages which shows every detail of his earnings and deductions. It is advisable to check this carefully as mistakes are made occasionally and if this has happened the mistakes should be rectified before the seaman signs off.

As has been pointed out above, if the sum of wages due to the seaman exceeds £50 and it is not practicable to pay the whole amount to him at the discharge, not less than £50, nor less than one quarter of the amount due, as shown in the account of wages, must be paid. Any remaining balance is then payable within seven days. Wages must be paid in cash unless the seaman has agreed to payment being made by cheque, money order, or direct to a bank or giro account. Such agreement should be confirmed in writing. Balances of wages can no longer be forwarded to a Mercantile Marine Office selected by the seaman.

At the pay-off, registered seafarers are given forms which tell them where and when to report at the end of their leave. A seafarer may also be entitled to free travel, in which case he will be given a railway warrant if he is being discharged at a port other than that at which he was engaged. It is usual for a representative of the National Union of Seamen to be present at this time to hear any grievances and to see that union dues have been paid; most seamen agree to have the latter deducted from their wages in the same way as national insurance and income tax.

At this time the seaman will have all his documents returned to him. The discharge book will have been filled in with details of the voyage and his insurance card is usually franked with 'Insurance paid by schedule s.s. . . . . . ' for every week in which contributions have been paid. The date to which the contributions have been paid is also indicated on his account of wages. On joining his next ship he should be able to produce this pay-off slip as proof of payment. If he has been paid up to a date in advance of joining the ship, he will not have to pay until that date is reached.

When leave has been completed, the seafarer who is not established in employment with a particular company should report back to the Merchant Navy Establishment Administration for further employment. If he wishes to take extra unpaid leave he must inform the Administration because should he fail to report within three months of his leave finishing his registration as a seafarer may be terminated.

When reporting for employment he should have in his possession his discharge book, identity card, and union book as well as his national insurance card and his last account of wages. Unemployment benefit is paid out at many offices of the MNEA but it should be borne in mind that if an insurance card is not presented regularly to an appropriate Department of Employment representative for franking during a period of unemployment then this could lead to a loss of benefit as well as the expense of buying insurance stamps for the weeks that have been missed.

It is advisable to keep the accounts of wages. They contain a record of sea service, earnings, income tax deductions, social security contributions and more often than not membership contributions to the appropriate union or association.

Should there be a dispute about any of these payments at any time the accounts of wages may become important material evidence. For those who make a lifetime career of seafaring, the accounts of wages may be the means of establishing rights to a pension, or a redundancy or medical severance payment.

6 Merchant Navy Institutions

Many of these bodies are commonly referred to by their initials, eg NUS, NMB, ILO, DoT.

Apostleship of the Sea (Stella Maris), Anchor House, Barking Road, London E16 4HB. Roman Catholic society providing clubs and other facilities for seafarers of all faiths.

Baltic Exchange, 14–20 St Mary Axe, London EC3A 8BU. The full title is the Baltic Mercantile and Shipping Exchange Ltd. Originating in one of London's 17th-century coffee houses, it is the world's largest market for the chartering (hiring) of ships of all nationalities. Shipbrokers and merchants' representatives meet 'on the Baltic' to arrange the chartering of ships, or space in ships, for the carriage of all kinds of goods to and from all parts of the world. Other classes of business transacted on the Baltic include the chartering of air transport and the purchase and sale of grain and oilseeds.

British Sailors' Society (BSS), Commercial Union House, 406–410 Eastern Avenue, Ilford, Essex. Interdenominational society providing clubs and other facilities for seafarers. Personal Affairs Office (advice available at any time). Office hours telephone 01-554 6285. After hours or at weekends: 01-530 3355 or 01-554 5370.

College of the Sea. *see* Marine Society, the.

Department of Trade (DoT), Marine Division, Sunley House, 90–93 High Holborn, London WC1W 6LP. The DoT is responsible, through its Marine Division, for most governmental matters connected with merchant shipping. Under the Merchant Shipping Acts of 1894 and 1970 it administers regulations for marine safety and welfare, certifies loadlines, ensures that standards of safety are observed in ship construction, ensures the provision of adequate life-saving, fire-fighting and radio equipment, and deals with the discipline, professional standards, health and accommodation of seamen. Much of the work entailed is carried out by the marine survey and mercantile marine officers at the ports (see Mercantile Marine Offices). At Sunley House are the

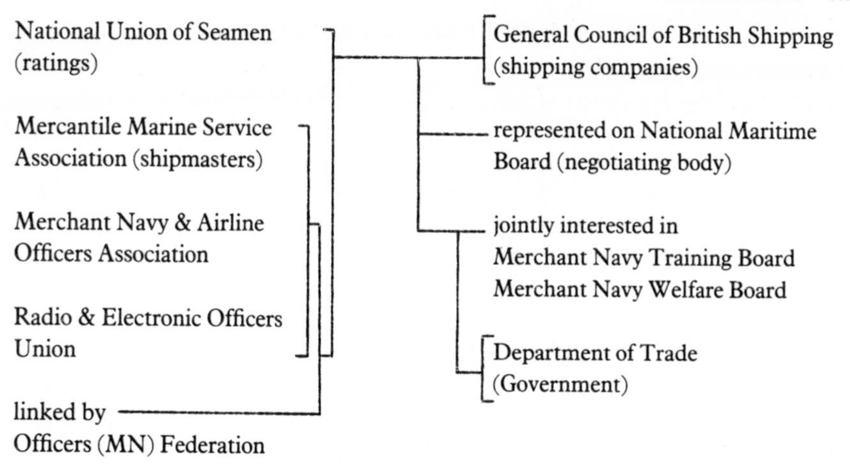

Fig 21 Some links between seafarers' associations, shipping companies, welfare organisations and Government.

Principal Examiner of Masters and Mates and the Chief Examiner of Engineers.

Dreadnought Seamen's Hospital, King William Walk, Greenwich, SE10 (telephone: 01-858 8111). Open day and night to all seafarers irrespective of creed or nationality. *See* Seamen's Hospital Society.

Flying Angel. *See* Missions to Seamen, The.

General Council of British Shipping (GCBS), 30–32 St Mary Axe, London EC3A 8ET. A body representative of British shipowners concerned with all policy issues including relations with government, labour relations and the regulation of employment throughout the Merchant Navy. It is responsible for the administration of the Merchant Navy Established Service Scheme, under which shipping companies engage crews. The GCBS is also responsible for the day-to-day operation of the National Sea Training Colleges set up for the purpose of training ratings for the deck and catering departments and as motormen. The British Shipping Careers Service operates under its auspices.

Honourable Company of Master Mariners, HQS *Wellington*, Temple Stairs, Victoria Embankment, London, WC2R 2PN. Founded in 1926, the Company was granted a Royal Charter in 1930 and became a Livery Company of the City of London in 1932. Membership is limited to 600 British master mariners, the principal objects being to provide a body representative of the senior officers of the Merchant Navy for the purpose of developing and promoting the traditions of that service, and to encourage and maintain high and honourable standards of ability and professional conduct.

Inter-Governmental Maritime Consultative Organisation (IMCO), 101 Piccadilly, London Q1W 0RE. (In 1981 will become International Maritime Organisation–IMO– and move to Albert Embankment, London SE1.) Established in 1958 to provide machinery for co-operation among governments in the field of governmental regulation and practices relating to technical matters, including safety at sea; to consider matters concerning unfair restrictive practices, and any matters concerning shipping that might be referred to it by the United Nations.

International Cargo Handling Co-ordination Association (ICHCA), Abford house, 15 Wilton Road, London SW1 V1LX. The organisation's function is to increase efficiency and promote economy in the handling and movement of goods from the point of origin to the final destination in all modes and phases of the transport chain.

International Christian Maritime Association (ICMA), St Michael Paternoster Royal College Hill, London EC4R 2RL. Joint organisation representing Christian maritime societies. Employs Citizens Advice Bureau adviser on behalf of seafarers. Publishes free directory of seafarers' clubs throughout the world and (with The Marine Society) advisory booklet for young seafarers.

International Labour Organisation (ILO) London Branch Office, 87–91 New Bond Street, London W1. Established in 1919, and recognised in 1946 by the United Nations as a special agency, the ILO exists to help promote social justice and by international action to improve labour conditions and living standards, and to promote economic and social stability. The Joint Maritime Commission of the ILO deals with matters concerning seafarers and meets periodically between maritime sessions of the ILO Conference.

International Transportworkers Federation (ITF), 133–135 Great Suffolk Street, London SE1 1PD. Aims to protect the interests of seafarers and other transport workers in the widest sense through trade union activity and cooperation.

King George's Fund for Sailors, 1 Chesham Street, London SW1X 8NF. Founded in 1917 to provide financial support for organisations existing to help the seafarer and his dependents.

Liverpool Seamen's Welfare Centre, Room 22, Oriel Chambers, 14 Water Street, Liverpool 2. Founded in 1942; maintains a rehabilitation centre for merchant seamen at Summerlands, near Kendal, where the disabled or unfit may apply for training in the furniture workshops.

Lloyd's of London, Lime Street, London EC3M 7HA. Taking its name from Edward Lloyd's coffee-house, which was probably established in 1688, Lloyd's is a society of underwriters whose main business is marine insurance; it constitutes the world's leading marine insurance market.

Lloyd's Register of Shipping, 71 Fenchurch Street, London EC3M 4BS. Although it also originated in Lloyd's coffee-house in 1760, Lloyd's Register is distinct from Lloyd's of London. It is the world's leading ship classification society and, since its amalgamation with the British Corporation in 1949, the only British one. The organisation surveys and classifies ships with particular

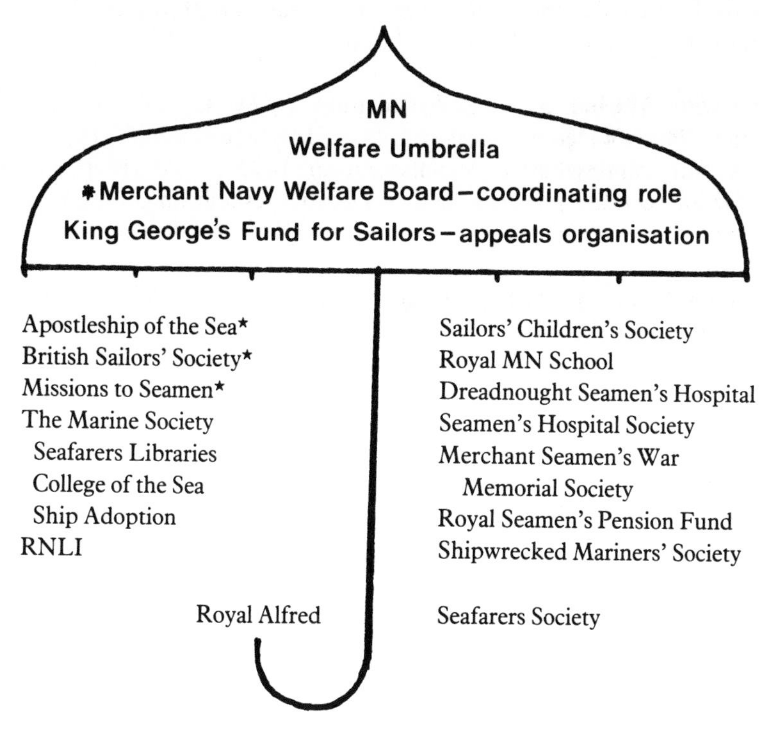

Fig 22 The Merchant Navy welfare umbrella

regard to their safety and operational efficiency, and a satisfactory Lloyd's classification is a guarantee to an underwriter that he may accept the risk of a vessel. The term 'A1' first appeared in 1775. The present symbol for a first-class vessel is – 100 A1.

Marine Society, The, 202 Lambeth Road, London SE1 7JW (telephone: 01-261 9535). Founded in 1756, now incorporates Seafarers Libraries, College of the Sea, Ship Adoption and London School of Nautical Cookery. Helps young people to go to sea; provides libraries and educational facilities for seafarers; puts schools in touch with seafarers; provides scholarships for ratings; teaches ships' cooks; etc.

Mercantile Marine Offices. These are to be found in the main ports in the United Kingdom, each under a Superintendent whose business it is to issue seamen with identity documents and certificates of efficiency and to receive fees for DoT examinations. The Superintendent may attend in an inspectorial capacity at the engagement of a crew and in the case of a wages dispute or disciplinary appeal at the discharge of a crew.

Mercantile Marine Service Association (MMSA), Nautilus House, Mariners' Park, Wallasey, Cheshire L45 7PH. Founded in 1857, the Association is the representative organisation of British shipmasters. It also administers certain charities and residential establishments for retired seafarers.

Merchant Navy and Airline Officers Association (MNAOA), Oceanair House, 750–760 High Road, Leytonstone, London E11 3BB. An association which represents the interests of navigating officers, engineer officers, cadets, pursers, catering officers and ship's surgeons as well as airline officers. (Likely to amalgamate with the REOU, *qv.*)

Merchant Navy Officers Pension Fund, Ebbisham House, Church Street, Epsom, Surrey LT17 4QF. A contributory fund established in 1938, and based on an NMB agreement to provide pensions for Merchant Navy officers.

Merchant Navy Training Board (MNTB), 30–32 St Mary's Axe, London EC3A 8ET. A voluntary organisation representative of shipping companies, seafarers' trade unions, nautical education and Government departments concerned. Its purpose is to keep under surveillance the whole field of training and associated further education for those making their career in the Merchant Navy. Various sections deal with deck, engineer, radio, catering and management and supervisory training, prepare training schemes and give training advice to the industry, to Government departments and to education authorities on the training of Merchant Navy personnel.

Merchant Navy Welfare Board, 19 Lancaster Gate, London W2 3LN. Incorporated in 1948 to promote co-operation between societies concerned with seamen's welfare; also maintains hotels and clubs for seafarers in certain ports, the Merchant Navy Hotel in London being at the headquarters address.

Merchant Seamen's War Memorial Society, Springbok Farm Training Centre, Alfold, Cranleigh, Surrey. Operates the Springbok Farm Training Centre; the purpose of the society is to help disabled seamen prepare themselves for employment as skilled tradesmen in the farming industry.

Missions to Seamen, The, St. Michael Paternoster Royal, College Hill, London EC4R 2RL. An Anglican organisation which has been caring for the spiritual and material welfare of seafarers since 1856. With 'Flying Angel' clubs in 87 ports, the society's chaplains are well known on ships of all nations.

National Maritime Board (NMB), 30-32 St Mary Axe, London EC3A 8ET. Established in 1917, and on a permanent basis in 1919, the Board is composed of equal numbers of representatives of the shipowners and seafarers and is responsible for all negotiations of wages and conditions of service in the Merchant Navy though, except by special arrangement, agreements do not apply to vessels under 200 tons gross or to certain other ships, including tugs and salvage vessels. Detailed working is carried on by a number of 'panels' representing the various interests of those forming the seafarers' part of the Board. A summary of agreements is published.

National Maritime Museum, Greenwich, London SE10 9NF. Britain's chief nautical museum; nearby is the clipper Cutty Sark and the Royal Naval College with its famous Painted Hall.

National Sea Training College. *See* General Council of British Shipping.

National Union of Seamen (NUS), Maritime House, Old Town, London SW4 0GP. Founded in 1887 by Havelock Wilson as the National Amalgamated Sailors' and Firemen's Union of Great Britain and Ireland. Today all seamen are required to be fully paid-up members before being signed on a British ship.

Nautical Institute. 202 Lambeth Road, London SE1 7JW. Constituted in 1972, the Institute is an independent professional body for qualified mariners directed by a Council, the majority of whom must be actively employed at sea. It promotes high standards, facilitates the exchange and publication of information and co-operates with other organisations to advance the education, training and practices of the nautical profession.

Officers (Merchant Navy) Federation. 750–760 High Road, Leytonstone, London E11 3BB. Body formed in 1928 to co-ordinate activites of all the officers' organisations, both at home and overseas. *See* Mercantile Marine Service Association, Merchant Navy and Airline Officers Association and Radio and Electronic Officers Union. (Disbanded 1980).

Port of London Authority (PLA). London Dock House, Thomas More Street, London E1 9AZ. A self-governing public trust established in 1908 to administer the docks and tidal waters of the river Thames.

Radio and Electronic Officers Union (REOU). 4–6 Branfill Road, Upminster, Essex RM14 2XX. Founded in 1912 to represent the interests of radio officers. (Likely to amalgamate with the MNAOA, *qv.*)

Royal Alfred Seafarers' Society. Weston Acres,Woodmansterne Lane, Banstead, Surrey SM7 3HB. Founded in 1865 for the relief of aged and disabled seamen; a principal function is to provide homes and flats for retired mariners, but a welfare officer is available at the society's headquarters from Monday to Friday, 9.30–4.30.

Royal Institute of Navigation, The. 1 Kensington Gore, London SW7 2AT. A scientific body whose object is to bring together all those interested in navigation, both air and sea. *The Journal of Navigation* is published three times yearly.

Royal Merchant Navy School, Bear Wood, Wokingham, Berkshire. Founded in 1827, the school was established to afford suitable relief to the orphans of seamen; in certain circumstances the school, which is residential, will now admit the sons of serving seafarers on a fee-paying basis. The Secretary will offer advice on the education of girls.

Royal National Life-boat Institution, 202 Lambeth Road, London SE1 7JW. Founded in 1824, the society exists to rescue life from shipwreck round the coasts of Great Britain and Ireland. The headquarters address is West Quay, Poole, Dorset.

Royal Seamen's Pension Fund, 58 High Street, Sutton, Surrey. Founded in 1911, the object of the fund is to provide supplementary pensions for British seafarers who have had long service in ships registered in the United Kingdom.

Sailors' Children's Society, Newland, Hull. Founded in 1821, the main function is to provide a home for the children of seafarers and to help orphans; children are admitted where the father is at sea and the mother is temporarily unable to care for them. Also maintains homes for retired seafarers.

Seamen's Hospital Society, 29 King William Walk, London SE10 9HX. At one time this society, which was founded in 1821, ran a group of seamen's hospitals, but nowadays it concerns itself with the welfare of seafarers and their dependents, particularly when ill or old.

Seafarers Libraries. *See* Marine Society, The.

Ship Adoption. *See* Marine Society, The.

Shipwrecked Mariners' Society, 1 North Pallant, Chichester, Sussex. Founded in 1839, the society exists to aid those shipwrecked upon British coasts and also their dependents.

Trinity House (The Corporation of). Tower Hill, London EC3N 4DH. Granted charter by Henry VIII in 1514, the corporation has even earlier origins. It the general lighthouse authority for England, Wales and the Channel Islands and the chief pilotage authority for England and Wales. The brethren are divided into younger and elder. The former must be master mariners before election and their position is almost entirely one of distinction; the elder brethren are divided into active and honorary, the former salaried officers with long experience in the Royal or Merchant Navy who control the business of the Corporation and who must be younger brethren before selection, and the latter ranging from members of the royal house to distinguished politicians. There are also Trinity Houses of Newcastle upon Tyne and Kingston upon Hull, of similar antiquity and still engaged in nautical affairs, notably pilotage.

United Nations Conference on Trade and Development (UNCTAD). Palais des Nations, 1211 Geneva 10, Switzerland. A United Nations organisation established in 1964 to promote international trade, especially with a view to speeding the economic development of developing countries.

Watch Ashore, The. Oceanair house, 750–760 High Road, Leytonstone, London E1 13BB. An association of wives, mothers and widows of Merchant Navy officers, and others, to further public interest in the British Merchant Navy. Also organises social functions and meetings.

7 Merchant Navy Terms

. . . there is hardly any recent book on shipping . . . which does not include a glossary of terms.
René de Kerchove

AB Able Seaman. To obtain a certificate of competency as AB a seaman must be over 18 and must have served three years on deck, with a maximum remission of six months for pre-sea training. He must also have passed an oral qualifying examination (see EDH), and must produce a steering certificate and a certificate of efficiency as Lifeboatman.

The examinations are normally taken at the National Sea Training College but the time at sea must also be served before the certificate is awarded.

Adrift A ship is said to be adrift when she has broken away from her moorings, so is a seaman who does not return to his ship at the expiry of his leave. The term is also used to describe gear which has broken away from a secured position, or even something missing from its usual place.

Agent One who represents a shipping company, or other organisation, in places where it has no establishment of its own. Shipowners normally appoint agents in places where they trade regularly and they act on behalf of the owners in all business matters.

Annual load line survey A survey conducted each year by a classification society surveyor to determine whether the ship's load line certificate should remain in force.

Anticyclone A region in which the barometric pressure is high relative to its surroundings. Although various conditions may be associated with it, it usually gives fine settled weather in the British Isles in summer. *See* Cyclone.

Arrest The detention of a ship which has broken the law or is in debt.

Automation The quality of being automatic or of acting mechanically only. Used in ships chiefly of devices which allow of automatic control of ship's equipment, particularly the remote control of the ship's engines.

Average (particular and general). Terms used in marine insurance. Particular average is when a partial loss arises caused by a peril insured against, and which is not a general average loss. General average occurs when action is taken, such as jettisoning cargo, for the good of the ship and all those concerned with the voyage. In the latter case shipowners and cargo owners contribute towards the expenses in proportion to their share in the voyage.

Backing A wind backs when its direction changes in an anti-clockwise direction. *See* Veering.

Ballast Material carried solely for purposes of stability. Once stones, sand and similar materials were used, but now it is almost invariably water carried in tanks designed for the purpose. *See* In Ballast *and* Flying Light.

Barratry A wrongful act wilfully committed by the master or crew to the prejudice of the owner or charterer.

Beaufort scale A scale of wind forces estimated on a numerical scale ranging from 0, calm, to 12, hurricane, first adopted by Admiral Beaufort in the early nineteenth century. As used today the wind speed is estimated from its effect on the condition of the sea.

Bill of health Document issued by the Port Medical Officer which gives a statement of the health conditions prevailing in the port or on board the ship.

Bill of lading A document signed by the master, or agent, on behalf of the owner for goods received on board ship. It is also a document of title which means that the person holding the bill is the owner of the goods mentioned on it.

Blue ensign British merchant ships normally wear the red ensign but may wear the blue ensign instead where the master and, in certain circumstances, one other officer are members of the Royal Naval Reserve, provided that the master has obtained his warrant from the Secretary of State for Defence.

Board of Trade sports Slang expression for boat-drill and fire-fighting practice, dating from the days when the Board of Trade fulfilled the functions now served by the Department of Trade.

Bond Essentially a promise or obligation. 'An Englishman's word is his bond.' The term is most frequently used at sea in connection with bonded goods, ie goods on which customs duty has not yet been paid.

The 'master's bond' is commonly used to refer to the goods, mainly tobacco and spirits, which he is allowed to sell duty free when the ship is outside territorial waters. The same term also has a technical use, unconnected with the above, when it refers to a bond which the master of an emigrant ship is required to enter into.

BORO Bulk/oil/Ro/ro. *See* Ro/ro and OBO.

Breaking bulk The act of beginning to discharge cargo.

Broken stowage Space lost when loading cargo caused by irregular sizes of packages and containers.

Broker A middleman between buyer and seller. Thus insurance broker; ship broker; chartering broker, etc.

Bulker or **bulk-carrier** Vessel which carries cargo in bulk, eg, sugar, bauxite, iron ore, etc.

Bumboat Small craft which trades with the crew.

Bunker Space in which the fuel is stowed. The fuel itself is usually referred to as 'bunkers'.

Cable One-tenth of a nautical mile. Strictly speaking this is 608 feet when referring to a standard nautical mile of 6080 feet, but it is usually taken as being 600 feet. The anchor chain is also called cable.

Cadet A cadet–a seafarer under training to be an officer–signs the ship's articles and is not bound by indentures as apprentices used to be, though he may be bound by some form of agreement with the shipowner.

Camber The convex curvature of the deck. Usually about one fiftieth of the beam.

Cancelling date The day on which the charterer may cancel the charter if the ship has not arrived at the loading port or is otherwise unable to begin loading at the prescribed time.

Cargo battens Also known as 'sparring', these are wooden battens fixed in the holds to keep the cargo away from bare steel and possible damage.

Certificate of registry Document carried on board the ship which is issued when the ship is first registered and shows details of the ship and its registered number.

Channel money Payment made to the crew at a paying off port before they receive the balance of their wages. This payment is usually made if the ship is not paying off on the day of arrival and enables the crew to pay customs duty, etc.

Channels To have the channels is to hanker for home; all but the most hardened seamen experience this feeling on approaching the English Channel, from which the expression derives, after a long voyage.

Charterer A person who hires a ship.

Charter party The contract between the charterer and the shipowner which sets out the terms on which the ship is hired. The principal types of charter are: voyage, time, bareboat and demise. As the name implies, voyage charter means that the ship is hired to make one voyage for the charterer. A time charter is for a specified period during which time the vessel may go anywhere and carry such cargoes as the terms of the charter allow. Bareboat and demise mean almost the same things in connection with cargo ships. Here the charterer takes over the ship in its entirety, provides his own crew, and runs the ship as part of his own fleet. However, demise chartered tankers are usually operated by their owners as a unit of the charterer's fleet.

Check weighing This is instituted when there is a dispute as to the weight of the cargo.

Classification The act of being registered with a society (eg Lloyd's Register of Shipping) which sets certain standards for the construction of the vessel. This implies that the ship measures up to these standards and indicates to all interested parties that she is a first-class ship. Although registration with a society is in no way obligatory it is of such benefit to the owner that nearly all ships of any size are so classified. The classification societies usually assign the load line. Registration with a classification society should not be confused with the compulsory registration of all British ships. *See* Certificate of registry *and* Port of registry.

Clean Apart from its conventional use this refers to documents, such as bills of lading and mate's receipts, which have not had any adverse comments about the condition of the goods written on them. Documents which have been endorsed with such remarks are classed as dirty, unclean or foul.

Clearance Official permission from the customs to leave a port.

Cofferdam A double watertight bulkhead, usually one frame wide, separating one double bottom tank from the next. It eliminates contamination by leakage from an oil fuel or sea water ballast tank into a fresh water tank.

Coffin plate The after plate of the keel where it is dished out to make a connection with the stern frame.

Cold front The boundary line between advancing cold air and a mass of warmer air under which the cold air pushes like a wedge. This occurs at the rear of a depression and is associated with heavy rain followed by showers and improving conditions.

Collision bulkhead An athwartship bulkhead, situated at least one-twentieth of the ship's length from the stem and intended to protect the main part of the vessel in the event of damage to the bow.

Commis waiter Assistant waiter.

Complement The total number of crew required to man a ship.

Conference lines Groups of shipping companies in given trades which operate in conjunction to guarantee a regular service at fixed rates.

Consul Official representative of a country who resides abroad and facilitates business relations between the two countries. The British consul in ports abroad acts in much the same way as a Mercantile Marine superintendent, and in larger ports there is often a shipping section attached to the consulate.

Containerisation The process of packing cargo in large boxes or containers to facilitate handling.

Containership; cellular containership Vessel designed to carry containers.

Contraband Goods upon which payment of customs duty has been illegally avoided.

Courtesy flag National flag of country which a ship is visiting, flown at the foremast head or on the yardarm as a mark of respect.

COW Crude Oil Washing Technique to clean a tanker's cargo tanks by recirculating the crude oil cargo through the tank washing machines. This operation takes place during cargo discharge and prevents sludge build-up on tank sides and in the bottom of cargo tanks. An anti-pollution measure which also improves the quantity of cargo discharged.

Cyclone Name given to a region of low barometric pressure. In temperate latitudes the cyclone is usually spoken of as a depression and the term is usually used to refer to cyclonic storms. *See* Tropical revolving storm *and* Anticyclone.

DBS Distressed British Seaman–one left abroad for repatriation by British authorities, not necessarily in any kind of distress.

Deadfreight Money which has to be paid for cargo space which has been booked and not used.

Decca Navigator Low-frequency aid to coastal navigation in which position fixes are obtained by plotting the readings from the phase-meters (Decometers) on a lattice grid.

Demurrage The compensation paid to a shipowner by the charterer when his ship is delayed beyond the stipulated time for loading or discharge.

Dhobying Washing clothes.

DHU Abbreviation for deck hand uncertificated. This rating is often given to men who first join the Merchant Navy over normal entry age. They can usually sit for the EDH certificate after 12 months' service.

Doc A slang expression for the cook deriving from the fact that he often treated the crew for minor ailments in sailing-ship days.

Dock dues Payment for the use of dock and port facilities.

Donkeyman An engine-room petty officer, the name deriving from the donkey-engine; among other things he tends the auxiliary engines in port.

DoT Department of Trade, formerly Department of Trade and Industry, and before that Board of Trade.

Draught or draft The depth to which a ship sinks in water, indicated by draught marks fore and aft.

Drawback The customs duty which is repaid when certain classes of goods, upon which duty has already been paid, are exported.

Dunnage Material, usually wood, which is used to separate items of cargo and to keep them away from the bare steel of the hold.

EDH Efficient Deck Hand: term used to describe a seaman who has taken his EDH examination successfully; he must be at least 18, have spent twelve months on deck, and have a stated amount of steering experience. Efficient Deck Hands serve in a capacity similar to that of AB.

Engineer Superintendent The shipping company official responsible for specifications for all ship's machinery and for the supervision of surveys and repairs on machinery; normally in charge of engine department personnel.

Entering inwards The process of reporting a newly berthed ship at the Custom House; except in very exceptional circumstances, this must be done by the master.

ERS Engine room storekeeper, of petty officer rank.

Established Service Scheme Under this scheme all British seafarers become Registered Seafarers and, with the exception of seasonal workers, are entitled to Establishment Benefit if they report available for employment, if they are sick, or if given leave to attend an approved training course. A Registered Seafarer and a shipping company may enter into a Company Service Contract.

Farmer In a 3-man watch, one may steer for two hours, one be on lookout and one stand-by; in the second two hours another steers; the one who does not steer in this watch is 'the farmer'.

Fathom A thousandth part of a nautical mile–six feet. A rough and ready measure from fingertip to fingertip with arms outstretched. A fathom of timber is a stack measuring 6 × 6 × 6 feet.

Feeder A large wooden box or hopper, constructed in the 'tween-deck above a hold which is filled with bulk grain. The bottom of the feeder is open to the lower hold and it is filled, or partly filled, with grain which will run down and take up any space caused by the settlement of the hold cargo.

Flag of convenience If a shipowner registers his ships in a country other than his own to escape paying some home taxation, to employ labour cheaper than that at home, or to benefit financially in any similar way, his ships are said to fly a flag 'of convenience'. The flags of Panama, Liberia and Honduras have been used for this purpose, hence the term 'Panlibhon'. The American terms 'flag of necessity' and 'runaway flag' have the same meaning.

Flag discrimination This term denotes the practice of reserving trade to the ships of a particular country or countries.

Flare The concavity of the bow section; also signal light used at sea.

FLASH Feeder Lighter Aboard Ship. *See* LASH.

Floors Deep vertical plates which run across the bottom of the ship from the centre line to the bilge.

Flying light An expression sometimes used to refer to a ship, empty of cargo, which is well out of the water.

Fog locker This is a mythical place used to confuse first trippers.On the whole it would be unwise for a first tripper to reveal that he knows it is a myth and to deprive others of their simple pleasure. *See* Green oil, Golden rivet *and* Long stand.

Foreign-going A foreign-going ship is one that trades beyond the home trade limits. *See* Home trade.

Founder To fill with water and sink.

Freeboard The vertical distance between the waterline and the upper edge of the deckline.

Flotsam Goods cast or lost overboard which are recoverable by reason of their remaining afloat. *See* Jetsam.

Freight Money paid for carrying cargo.

Freight ton A ton of cargo either 40 cubic feet or 2,240 lbs. The shipowner usually has the option of charging freight on whichever will give him the greater return. Thus heavy cargo, when one ton occupies less than 40 cu ft of space, will be charged on weight; and bulky cargo, where 40 cu ft weighs less than one ton, will be charged on volume.

Front The line of separation between warm and cold masses of air, usually accompanied by rainfall and a change of wind. *See* Depression *and* Cold *and* Warm front.

Galley A ship's kitchen.

Garboard strake The line of bottom plating next to the keel.

Gearless bulker One without derricks or cranes, thus dependent on shore equipment for loading and discharging.

GP General purpose: term used to describe crew in which there is no division between deck and engine-room ratings; ratings are graded according to experience and seniority GP1, GP2 and GP3.

Graving dock The correct term for a dry dock which has been excavated. The term dry dock also refers to a floating dock.

Greaser Engine-room rating, now motorman.

Green flash Sometimes seen very briefly at the moment of sunrise or sunset, appearing as a green or bluish colouration of the upper part of the sun; also seen as a ray of green light shot up from the sun at sunset. There is controversy over whether it exists or is merely an optical illusion.

Green oil This is not required for the starboard sidelight which has a green glass filter and uses quite ordinary oil. Green oil is sought only by green sailors. *See* Fog locker.

Golden rivet This is reputed to be at the end of the shaft tunnel and is revered by all engineers. As in the case of fog locker, allow them to have their fun.

Gudgeon Protruding sockets on rudder and sternframe which carry the steel pins (pintles) on which the rudder pivots.

Heaving The vertical lifting of the whole ship in heavy seas.

Hogging When the ends of a ship are lower in the water than the 'midship portion. This condition tends to be caused by loading too much cargo in the ends of the ship, or when the middle of the ship is suspended on the crest of a large wave. *See* Sagging.

Home trade This phrase referred to voyages made within the limits of the British Isles and the range of ports between the river Elbe in Germany and the port of Brest in France. The terms of a Home Trade agreement used to be rather different from those of a Foreign-going one.

IDF Inter-departmental flexibility: term used to describe crew in which members of different departments can be called upon to help with tasks in departments other than their own.

IG Inert Gas System whereby engine consumption gases are cleaned, cooled and distributed under pressure to cargo tanks in a tanker to displace oxygen and eliminate the risk of fire and explosion.

In ballast A ship is said to be 'in ballast' when she is carrying ballast only and no cargo.

Intercostal Literally 'between the ribs'; in a ship, refers to anything fitted between the frames or floors.

International Collision Regulations Rules which lay down the lights and shapes which must be carried, the sound signals which should be used and the action which should be taken so that a ship avoids collision.

Jetsam Goods cast or lost overboard which are recoverable through being washed ashore. *See* Flotsam.

Jettison To throw overboard cargo or equipment for the safety of the ship. *See* Average.

JOS Junior Ordinary Seaman: a deck boy who is at least 16½ and who has been at sea for up to nine months; towards the nine months there is an allowance of up to one-half (but not exceeding six months in all) of the time spent in sea school, but he must have completed one voyage. The term Junior Seaman is replacing this term. *See* SOS, EDH and AB.

Knot A unit of speed, being one nautical mile of 6,080 feet steamed in one hour. The speed is always expressed as so many knots and it is incorrect to refer to the speed as knots per hour.

Laden in bulk When the cargo is loose or in bulk in the way that grain is usually carried.

Lagan Goods cast overboard which are buoyed so that they can be recovered.

Lamptrimmer The deck storekeeper; among his responsibilities is the keeping of oil lamps trimmed and ready for use. This term is becoming outmoded.

LASH Lighter Aboard Ship system: used to describe ships designed to carry barges loaded with cargo. Such systems are independent of shore facilities for loading and discharging, offering dramatic reductions of turn-round time. See FLASH.

Lay days The days allowed in the charter party for the loading or discharge of cargo.

LEFO Abbreviation meaning that a ship is bound to Land's End 'for orders', meaning that she will receive orders concerning ports of discharge while en route, or on arrival off Land's End.

Lifeboatman's certificate or lifeboat certificate. Part of the EDH examination, but a certificate also available to other seafarers, this is a qualification in boat work. By law each passenger ship must carry a certain number of certificated lifeboatmen.

Light dues Toll levied on ships for the purpose of maintaining lighthouses, lightships and buoys around the coast.

Liper Hybrid of LIner and tramPER.

Lloyd's agent An agent of the Corporation of Lloyd's. *See* Chapter 6.

Lloyd's surveyor A surveyor employed by Lloyd's Register of Shipping. *See* Chapter 6.

LNG Liquefied natural gas, hence LNG carrier.

Log An instrument for computing the speed of the ship and the distance run. Also the official record book. To log a man is to enter his name and offence in the official log; hence the expression 'to be logged'. *See* Official log.

Long stand What it says. *See* Fog locker.

Loran Low-frequency, long-range electronic aid to navigation covering parts of the North Atlantic, Arctic, Mediterranean and North Pacific Oceans. The ground-wave signal gives accuracy of half a mile up to a range of 1,000 miles.

LPG Liquefied petroleum gas, hence LPG carrier.

Marine Superintendent The shipping company official generally responsible to the management for all matters relating to the officers and crew and also for the maintenance and supply of all deck department gear; usually former navigating officer. Larger companies will also employ an Engineer Superintendent and a Catering Superintendent.

Master The officer in command of a merchant ship. The term 'Captain', which is invariably used as a form of address, is a courtesy title.

Mate's receipt Document given and signed by the mate in return for cargo received on board. Unlike the bill of lading, which is subsequently issued to the person holding a mate's receipt, it is not a document of title.

Mayday International distress signal.

Mean nautical mile One of 6,076.91 feet.

Monsoon Term originally referring to the winds of the Arabian Sea which blow for about six months from the north-east and for about six months from the south-west. Today the term is also used to refer to other winds which occur persistently and with regularity at certain times of the year.

MPT Ministry of Posts and Telecommunications.

Notice of readiness Formal notice given by the master to the charterer, or his agent, that the ship is, in all respects, ready to load cargo.

OBO Ore-bulk-oil, hence OBO carriers, ships which can carry these cargoes.

Official log A record book kept by the master in which he must, by law, enter certain particulars relating to the ship and its voyage. This book has to be handed in to a Mercantile Marine Superintendent at the end of the voyage.

Official number The number issued to the ship upon being registered. It is the number 'carved' on the beam of the ship. This is a legal requirement and has nothing to do with being registered with a classification society. *See* Classification.

OMEGA Very low-frequency radio-navigation system using position lines produced by phase-difference measurements from ground transmitters; should give positional accuracy within 1–2 nautical miles.

On survey A survey at which both the owner and the charterer are represented which takes place immediately prior to the ship going on charter. At the end of the charter another survey is held. This is called the 'off survey' and a comparison of the results will give an indication of what damage has been done to the ship during the period of the charter.

OO Ore-oil, hence OO carriers. *See* OBO.

Peggy A messman; usually a deck boy new to the sea whose main job is cleaning and tidying the men's quarters. Now somewhat archaic.

Pilot Defined by the Merchant Shipping Act as any person not belonging to a ship who has the conduct thereof. He is an authorised person engaged to advise on the navigation of the ship in and out of the port and in other confined waters.

Pitching A ship pitches when she rises and falls alternately at the bow and stern, as distinct from rolling from side to side.

Port of registry The port where the ship is registered. It is the port whose name appears on the stern.

Pounding The slamming of the forefoot, or underside of the bow, in heavy weather. It usually produces a jarring sensation which shakes the whole ship.

Pratique The official recognition that the ship is healthy which allows it to make contact with the shore. The meaning of the yellow 'Q' flag is: 'My ship is healthy and I request free pratique'. This flag should be hauled down as soon as the request has been granted.

Proper return port This phrase may mean any of the following: (1) The port where a seaman was shipped. (2) A port in the country to which the seaman belongs. (3) A port agreed to by the seaman at the time of his discharge.

Pumpman Rating of petty officer rank employed in many tankers.

Record book A book which records a planned programme of training at sea, applicable to cadets and junior ratings.

Red oil *See* Green oil.

Reefer Refrigerated cargo vessel.

Riggers A shore gang who rig derricks, warp a ship from berth to berth, and generally do the work of the ship's deck seamen in the home port when the sailing crew has been paid off. Also used in its more correct sense to mean men who work in a rigging loft and set up rigging.

Ro/ro Roll-on/roll-off: used to describe ships designed to carry vehicles which can be driven on and off the vessel.

Rummaging The searching of a ship for contraband by customs officers. These are known as 'rummagers' or 'rummaging officers'.

Runners Crew employed to take the ship from one port to another only. Also the working wires on derricks.

Sagging When the middle of the ship is lower in the water than the ends. this tends to be caused by loading an excess of cargo in the middle hatches of a ship with engines aft or when the ends of a ship are supported by the crests of large waves. *See* Hogging.

Salvage Money paid for the saving of a ship and/or cargo, or the property that has been saved.

Seabee Barge-carrying system (see LASH) where the mothership is lowered as a floating dock to float barges on or off.

Seaworthiness A ship is seaworthy when she is reasonably fit in all respects to encounter the ordinary perils of the sea.

Shackle Length of anchor cable, Merchant Navy 15 fathoms, Royal Navy 12 fathoms; normal ships have about 9 shackles on each anchor, VLCCs about 13.

Sheer The rise of the deck forward and aft as compared with amidships.

Sheer strake A heavy line of plating along the ship's side at main deck level.

Shelter deck ship Provided that certain regulations are complied with, the deck above the tonnage deck can be recognised as an 'open space' and exempted from tonnage measurement and dues. In the conventional shelter deck ship this forms the upper 'tweendeck. The tonnage hatch and the openings in the 'tweendeck bulkheads are among the main features of the requirements.

Shifting boards Temporary bulkheads erected in the hold to prevent the free flow of cargoes, such as grain, when the vessel is in heavy weather.

Short ton One of 2,000lbs; invariably used on American ships.

Shut out Used of part of a consignment that is not loaded, either because there is no room or because the ship is due to sail at a given time.

Signal letters A set of four letters allocated to ships and used for recognition purposes in both radio and visual signalling. British ships' letters begin with either G or M.

Slops Clothes and other goods for sale on board ship, hence *slop chest* or place of sale; cf *bond*.

Smoke-O Tea break.

SOS Senior Ordinary Seaman: a deck boy who is at least 17½ and who has completed eighteen months' sea service. Now likely to be Seaman Grade II. *See* JOS. Also a distress signal.

Squall A relatively strong wind that rises suddenly, lasts for a few minutes, and then dies away comparatively quickly.

Stemming To stem a tide or current is to face it. Also the act of booking a ship for drydock, bunkers or cargo.

Stevedore Strictly this is someone employed in loading a ship, but it is generally used to describe anyone loading or discharging cargo.

Stowage factor How many cubic feet a ton of cargo occupies inclusive of broken stowage.

Surveyor An expert who examines various parts of the ship or cargo. Ships are subjected to a great variety of surveys by many different surveyors representing widely differing interests. Ships classified by Lloyd's Register of Shipping are surveyed annually; this survey is usually held concurrently with the load line survey which Lloyd's surveyors are also empowered to conduct. Lloyd's also hold more detailed surveys every four years. Safety surveys are carried out by DoT surveyors and radio surveys by MPT surveyors. There are also surveys carried out by surveyors acting on behalf of the owners and charterers.

Swell Wave motion in the ocean caused by a disturbance which is likely to persist long after the original disturbance has ceased. It is quite common for there to be a swell coming from a different direction from the waves caused by the wind.

Tally A record made of cargo loaded or discharged.

Teu Twenty-foot equivalent units. A measure of the capacity of container ships.

Tonne Metric ton of 1,000 kilogrammes or 2,204.62lbs.

Tornado The same term refers to different conditions in different parts of the world. In West Africa it is a squall which accompanies a thunderstorm. The other kind, most commonly found in the central plains of the Mississippi region, is a very violent counter-clockwise whirl averaging only a few hundred feet across and giving rise to winds which have exceeded 200mph. This is also called a 'twister'.

Trade winds Constant winds which blow from the tropical high pressure belts towards the equatorial regions of low pressure. They blow from a north-easterly direction in the northern hemisphere and from a south-easterly direction in the southern hemisphere.

Tropical revolving storm A small area of intense low pressure around which winds of hurricane force blow. These storms give rise to violent conditions and whenever possible ships try to keep away from them. They are also known in various parts of the world as cyclones, hurricanes, typhoons, and willy-willies. *See* Cyclone.

Turn to Begin work.

ULCC Ultra-large crude carrier (of oil). Tankers of 300,000 deadweight tons and over are so classified.

Ullage The amount by which a container is short of being full. It is usually heard at sea in connection with tanks.

Underwriter Person who takes an insurance risk. So called because he writes his name under the terms of the policy.

Veering A wind veers when the direction it blows from changes in a clockwise direction. The same term also means to pay out cable or rope.

VLCC Very large crude carrier (of oil), under 300,000 deadweight tons.

Warm front The boundary between the cold air mass in a depression and the following warm air mass. It is usually deep in extent and brings with it continuous rain or snow.

Warp To tow or move a ship by a line attached to a buoy or bollard on the quayside; the motive power is usually the windlass at the bow and a warping or mooring winch at the stern. Also a mooring rope used for warping.

WNA Abbreviation for Winter North Atlantic, a load line applicable in certain circumstances (*See* Chap. 1).

Yaw To deviate from a course by swinging from side to side.

8 Further Reading

If there is any doubt about Britain being a maritime nation, at least the volume of literature on maritime subjects should dispel it.
HRH the Duke of Edinburgh

Everything about a Ship and its Cargo, the English translation of a German book by Friedrich Böer, is detailed and attractively illustrated, with a number of excellent 'cut-through' drawings. Unfortunately, it was published privately and is hard to come by. Complementary to it is P M Alderton's *Sea Transport: Operation and Economics*, a book which explains what different types of merchant ship do and how they are managed.

Neil Mostert's *Supership* provides an intelligent outsider's view of life aboard a VLCC, while an inside view is given by Captain S J Harland's *The Dustless Road*. Although written for a 'career' series of books, the latter is a straightforward autobiography by a modern professional seafarer. Similar material in pamphlet form, describing particular jobs at sea or particular voyages, is available from Ship Adoption, a department of The Marine Society. Although some years old, Jan de Hartog's vignettes, gathered together in *A Sailor's Life*, provide an insight into those realities of life in the Merchant Navy which do not change much from one generation to another. For the young person about to go to sea Leo Madigan's booklet *Random Jottings for Young Seafarers* (available from The Marine Society) might be described as essential reading.

Edward P Harnack's *All About Ships and Shipping* is a handbook of popular nautical information, as is T A Hamptom's *The Sailor's World*, subtitled 'an easy guide to ships, harbours and customs of the sea'. In much the same vein, though arranged as a one-volume encyclopaedia, is *The Oxford Companion to Ships and the Sea*. All these works have a Royal Navy orientation though also containing information applicable to merchant ships. A Ansted's *Dictionary of Sea Terms*, on the other hand, is inspired by commercial ships but has its roots in a long-past era of sailing vessels. It is particularly useful to those interested in the history of shipping.

This is not the place to recommend nautical textbooks, which are constantly being revised and updated, but a newcomer to the industry will probably want the *Seamanship Handbook for Basic Studies*, C H Wright's *The Efficient Deck Hand* and the Stanford Maritime publications *Basic Principles of Marine Navigation* and *Marine Chartwork and Navaids*. *A Seaman's Guide to the Rule of the*

Road is a programmed book specially designed for the student studying on his own. *Safety at Sea*, by ECB and Kenneth Lee, is more than a safety handbook –well worth reading for its historical content.

Talbot-Booth's Merchant Ships, in three volumes, is a vast and comprehensive directory of world merchant ships, with 8,500 profile drawings to scale and supplements to keep it up to date. Other books useful for identifying ships and ship types include Bert Moody's *Ocean Ships*, R Munro-Smith's *Merchant Ship Types* and Duncan Haws' *Merchant Fleets in Profile*. The latter is a three-volume work which offers an historical survey of the fleets of the past century or so.

To those who want to delve further into the past, Björn Landström's *The Ship* is recommended–a handsome book written and illustrated by a man who is both scholar and artist. Another handsome book, this one confined to the study of a particular era, is *The Great Age of Sail*, edited by Joseph Jobé. Right up to date, on the other hand, is *Ship's Cargo Cargo Ships*, edited by Henri Kummerman and Robert Jacquinet, a work which is concerned with the evolution and design of contemporary vessels and their prospects in the future. These three books are all of 'coffee-table' size, but they will serve the scholar well and between them present an accurate picture of shipping over a period of 3,000 years.

For those who want detailed information about modern shipping companies and their business, the annual publications *Directory of Shipowners, Shipbuilders and Marine Engineers*, published by *Marine Week*, and *Fairplay World Shipping Year Book* are indispensable reference books. There is considerable overlap, but the first gives ships' names and the second financial detail. Unique in its field and described by its title is J L Loughran's *A Survey of Mercantile Houseflags and Funnels*, though the *Journal of Commerce* also publishes a useful flags and funnels wall-chart.

Serious students of recent shipping history will need to seek out the *Report of the Committee of Inquiry into Shipping*, published in 1970, otherwise known as the Rochdale Report, and SG Sturmey's *British Shipping and World Competition*. J M M Hill's *The Seafaring Career* arose from the ferment excited by the Rochdale Committee and is a study of the forces which affect turnover among merchant seamen. Although concerned in part with specifically American problems, S A Lawrence's *International Sea Transport: The Years Ahead* will help to fill in the recent background.

Good histories of the Merchant Navy are rare. Richard Armstrong's three-volume history of seafaring, *The Early Mariners, The Discoverers* and *The Merchantmen*, is something of a pot-boiler. Grant Uden's two-volume *British Ships and Seamen* has some relevance, as have Christopher Lloyd's three books, *The British Seaman, Ships and Seamen* and *Atlas of Maritime History*.

The second of these is a feast of pictures and the third contains some fascinating maps. But C E Fayle's *A Short History of the World's Shipping Industry*, R H Thornton's *British Shipping*, Ralph Davis's excellent *The Rise of the English Shipping Industry in the 17th and 18th Centuries* and A G Course's *The Merchant Navy: a Social History* are all more specifically about merchant shipping. Knut Weibust's *Deep Sea Sailors*, a kind of social anthology derived largely from reminiscences, complements these where they cover the history of the past century or so.

Sailors' reminiscences provide some of the best reading. Barlow's *Journal*, edited in two volumes by Basil Lubbock, provides a vivid picture of the seaman's life in the 17th century. Captain Cook's *Journals*, edited by many people and notably by J C Beaglehole, will serve for the 18th century. The great work in the 19th century is R H Dana's *Two years before the Mast*. From the end of the 19th century right through to modern times the books are legion. Here are a few: Sir David Bone's *The Brassbounder* and *Landfall at Sunset*, A H Rasmussen's *Sea Fever*, Captain J W Holmes's *Voyaging* and the three-volume memoirs of Sir James Bisset, one-time commodore of Cunard, *Sail Ho!*, *Tramps and Ladies* and *Commodore*. Captain Harry Grattidge was also commodore of Cunard but confined himself to a single volume, the seamanlike and entertaining *Captain of the Queens*.

J Lennox Kerr edited the Second World War memoirs of a number of merchant seamen and these essays were published under the title *Touching the Adventures*. Shortly after that war Michael Page wrote *A Sea with Many Islands*, probably the best book of recent reminiscences, and the author of the present work has edited a collection of modern stories of the Merchant Navy at peace which were published under the title *Seamen and the Sea*. Other specifically Merchant Navy books with which the author has also been associated include *Twenty Singing Seamen*, a volume of merchant seamen's short stories, *Voices from the Sea*, a collection of merchant seamen's verse, *Spare Time at Sea*, intended for use on board ship, and *The Shoregoer's Guide to World Ports*, a traveller's guide written specifically for seafarers.

The Merchant Navy is well endowed with periodic literature–two daily newspapers, *Lloyd's List* and the *Journal of Commerce*; two weeklies, *Fairplay* and *Marine Week*; several monthlies, each a specialist: the *Nautical Magazine*, the oldest nautical miscellany, *Sea Breezes*, a magazine devoted mainly to old ships, *Seaways*, the journal of the Nautical Institute, *The Telegraph*, the excellent newspaper-format journal of the MNAOA, *The Seaman*, journal of the National Union of Seamen, and *Seatrade*, a business journal; one bimonthly, *The Sea*, in newspaper-format and produced for seafarers by The Missions to Seamen; a number of quarterlies, including *The Seafarer*, journal of The Marine Society, *The Marine Observer*, devoted to meteorology and oceanography, *The Mariner's Mirror*, journal of the Society for Nautical Research, *The Journal of Navigation*, issued by the Royal Institute of Navigation, and the *Journal* of the Honourable Company of Master Mariners; and an annual, *The Dog Watch* published by the Shiplovers' Society of Victoria, Australia, and distributed in the United Kingdom by The Marine Society. This list makes no mention of shipping company house journals and similar magazines, many of them of the highest quality.

The Marine Society is willing to advise anybody about books and journals concerned with the Merchant Navy, and such advice is free.